We Teach With Technology

New Visions for Education

Greg Kearsley
The George Washington University

Beverly Hunter
National Science Foundation

Mary Furlong
University of San Francisco

Franklin, Beedle & Associates, Incorporated
8536 SW St. Helens Drive, Suite D
Wilsonville, Oregon 97070 (503) 682-7668

Dedication

This book is dedicated to our students . . .
who have taught us so much.

Publisher: James F. Leisy, Jr.
Manuscript Editor: Sheryl Rose
Cover and Interior Design: Lisa Cannon
Photography: Mark Hooper
Manufacturing: Malloy Lithography

Library of Congress Cataloging-in-Publication Data

Kearsley, Greg,
We teach with technology : new visions for education / Greg Kearsley, Beverly Hunter, Mary Furlong.
p. cm.
Includes bibliographical references and index.
ISBN 0-938661-37-X
1. Computer -assisted instruction--United States. I. Hunter, Beverly. II. Furlong, Mary S. III. Title.
LB1028.5.K37 1992
371.3 34--dc20 91-44315
CIP

Preface

Computers and other instructional technology have long been heralded as change agents in our educational system. However, no form of technology since the chalkboard has really created a fundamental change in schools. Despite many impressive demonstrations over the years, technology has not lived up to its potential to improve learning for most students.

But something dramatic is beginning to happen in classrooms around the world. More and more teachers are using computers as tools to support their own work and their vision of what education is about. Teachers are discovering that computers can serve as electronic chalkboards, administrative aids, writing and publishing vehicles, information resources, communication pathways, data collection instruments, laboratory workbenches, and creative media. Once teachers begin to use computers routinely as personal and teaching tools, we see a more profound impact of technology in schools. The computer is no longer some sort of "learning aid" but an integral part of classroom activities.

This book tries to document the remarkable new direction of educational computing as seen through the eyes of teachers themselves. We studied exemplary computer-using teachers and how they use computers in their schools. We have tried to capture their insights, strategies, and feelings about the use of computers in the classroom.

We would like to acknowledge the enthusiastic cooperation received from all of the teachers whose stories make this book what it is. We would also like to thank the many individuals who reviewed drafts and made contributions, including Helayne Waldman, Lenny Schwartz and Janet Graeber. Finally, we would like to express our appreciation to Jim Leisy of Franklin, Beedle & Associates for his vision in publishing this book.

Contents

Chapter 1
Information Age Teachers

Teachers are playing key roles in helping the U.S. educational system make the transition from the Industrial Age to the Information Age. The teachers who contributed to this book represent a sampling of the thousands who are on the leading edge of this transition.

These teachers have developed or are in the process of developing their own vision of the direction schooling must take to meet the needs of the children of the Information Age, and they have a sense of mission about their roles in making the needed changes.

Since the territory they are exploring is in many respects uncharted, these teachers realize that they, like their students, are learners. They no longer believe they must play the role of authority and dispenser of knowledge at all times in their classrooms.

Because they are initiating changes in their schools, they are spending more and more of their time collaborating with other teachers, researchers, community leaders, and parents. The cross-disciplinary and project-oriented curriculum evolving for the Information Age requires more team teaching and coordination than the Industrial Age school demanded. These teachers seek real audiences for their students' work, which means closer connections with the world outside the school.

Information Age teachers are experimenting with innovative approaches to teaching. In the process, many of these teachers are reexamining their ideas about what learning is. They are seeing their students as actively constructing knowledge rather than as passive receivers of knowledge. Because they realize their students must become lifelong learners, they are expecting their students to take more responsibility for managing their own learning.

Some of the teachers in this book are discovering more ways to meet the needs of students from diverse cultural backgrounds. They are finding ways to help children build on their own out-of-school interests, experiences, and knowledge.

Teachers are developing new ways to manage their classes. Many are moving toward more small-group activities, and some are focusing on improving their skills in managing cooperative learning groups. They give fewer lectures and spend more time working with small groups and individual students.

These teachers are providing a wide range of materials, media, tools, and information sources for their students. Some are focusing on providing their students with access to information or expertise outside the classroom or school. They are less inclined to have their students fill out worksheets or answer textbook questions, and more likely to make assignments involving original investigations or writing for real audiences.

As their ideas about the nature of learning changes, they are developing alternative ways of assessing their students' learning progress. They are depending less on student performance on paper and pencil tests, and more on the quality and substance of students' oral and written communications.

The teachers contributing to this book are at different stages in their professional development and in their mastery of the computer-based tools of the Information Age. Some are just beginning to apply computer-based tools to their own work, and are introducing their students to computer applications that fit into the existing curriculum. Others tried many different technologies before they discovered how to match the tools with their own vision of learning and teaching. Many are taking leadership roles in their schools, districts, states, and professional societies. All are finding the teaching profession more rewarding as they become more active learners themselves.

These teachers are drawing on a wide range of resources and sources of support, from colleagues, the community, their administration, industry, or professional societies. They are learning how to overcome myriad obstacles to change—policies, curricula, tests, schedules, budgets, politics. In some areas, teachers and principals are being given increased responsibility for decision making. They are using technology as a means of restructuring schools to provide more relevant and effective instruction.

A New Philosophy for Educational Computing

Computers have been used for educational applications since the early 1960s. However, for the first three decades of educational computing, the major focus was programming and computer-assisted instruction—the use of the computer to provide curriculum materials in the form of drills, tutorials, games, and simulations.

With the emergence of personal computers and various types of application software in the 1980s, the primary use of computers in the classroom shifted from a content delivery device to a learning tool. Teachers and students began using word processing, desktop publishing, database, spreadsheet, telecommunications, graphing, and graphics programs. They also began experimenting with a new generation of educational software that encouraged critical thinking, problem solving, decision making, and exploration.

As teachers developed more experience with computers as learning and thinking tools, they realized that the computer could be a vehicle for restructuring curriculum and classroom practice. Instead of passive learning activities such as reading or following along on the chalkboard, students became active participants in computer-based projects, usually working in pairs or small groups.

Another important development in the 1980s was the realization that the computer could be a *teaching* tool as well as a learning tool. Teachers discovered they could assign problems to small groups of students sharing a computer. With the advent of inexpensive LCD panels, teachers began to use computers as electronic chalkboards to demonstrate ideas to the entire class. They also found that the use of telecommunications networks for electronic mail, bulletin boards, and to access online databases extended their range beyond the walls of the classroom. As teachers developed experience and confidence with a range of computer applications, they were better able to personalize the use of technology to support their own goals and style.

This book shows the great diversity in the ways teachers are employing computers and related technologies. This diversity mirrors the wide range of technology applications in the "real world"—from word processing and desktop publishing to large screen presentation aids, to scientific visualization tools, to computer-aided design, and to accessing databases via telecommunications networks.

Indeed, it is the desire to "recontextualize" learning that is driving many of the innovations in computer use in schools. Teachers are seeking ways of setting up learning environments that are more realistic than traditional classrooms. There are many reasons for this emphasis, including the obvious need to help students become better problem solvers. Computers and related technology can be used to help create realistic problem-solving situations, as well as providing tools to help pose and solve problems. For example, specially designed video stories are used to create realistic contexts in which students can pose as well as solve mathematical problems much more effectively than they can from text-based story problems (see Chapter 7). Similarly, students collaborating with distant peers via telecommunications are often working on real problems, such as the problem of how to improve local recycling efforts or control pollution (see Chapter 5).

Using computers as a teaching tool is a new and profound development in educational computing. We believe that this new perspective will ultimately unleash the full potential of computers in education. We also believe that it will allow many teachers to be much more productive, creative, and successful in their classrooms.

About This Book

This book differs from other books about educational computing in a number of ways. First, it is written from the point of view of teachers instead of the "expert" or "technologist" perspective. Rather than surveying all possible ways of using technology in school, the book presents teachers who are adopting and adapting technology to support their own goals and visions for the reform of teaching and learning in the Information Age. The book addresses the concerns of teachers, concerns such as:

- How can I make my classes more interesting to my students?
- How can I help my students become better problem solvers?
- How can I get my students to take more responsibility for their own learning?
- How can I get my students to work more cooperatively together?
- How can I help my students see the connection between school and their experiences outside school?
- How can I help students make connections among the skills and ideas they learn in various school subjects, rather than treating these skills and ideas as disconnected pieces of knowledge?
- How can I spend less time on "administrivia" and more time helping my students?

Unlike other books on educational computing, this book is organized according to curriculum domains. Each chapter focuses on a specific subject or computing activity, such as writing or telecommunications. Chapters begin with an overview of the topic that explains basic concepts and summarizes the current state of the art. Following the overview are a number of case studies or profiles of actual teachers organized around major topics or themes. Throughout the chapter you will find sections that describe specific programs or examples of applications mentioned in the overview or case studies.

There are many connections between the chapters in terms of concepts and applications. For example, a recurring theme is teachers' desire to provide real audiences for their students' work. Multimedia (e.g., videodisc or CD-ROM) is often used. Technology can break down the artificial barriers between subject areas, leading many teachers to adopt a cross-curriculum approach. These connections are mentioned as they occur and direct you to the related information in other chapters.

Who Is This Book For?

This book is written for teachers and prospective teachers who are seeking to change or improve their own classroom practice and to help our educational system make the transition to the Information Age. The focus of the book is on teaching in K-12 settings, although the book should also be useful to instructors at the college level, especially education faculty.

We believe this book will make a good text for elementary and secondary methods courses, as well as courses about educational technology. The book illustrates the connection between technology and current reforms in educational practice, such as cooperative and collaborative learning, contextualized learning, interdisciplinary learning, problem solving, higher-order thinking skills, information-handling skills, and alternative assessment. The book addresses a wide range of technology applications in schools and presents topics from a teacher's perspective. Each chapter includes activities that can be used as class assignments or for self-assessment.

This book assumes a modest degree of "computer literacy" and is intended for readers who already have some experience using computers. The focus is on the use of computers in teaching, not providing an introduction to computers. Although we provide explanations of many basic concepts in educational computing, it is not the purpose of this book to be either a primer or comprehensive textbook. There are many good books that do this already (see Chapter 14). Our goal is to present a different perspective on the field and provide a sourcebook of ideas that teachers can build on in their own classrooms.

About the Teachers in This Book

The teachers you will meet in this book represent a broad spectrum of backgrounds and personal views. They teach different subjects, different grade levels, at different kinds of schools (or nonschools), and in different places in the U.S. and other countries. The one thing they have in common is that they are using computers and related technology to support the kinds of change they see as needed for the Information Age.

The teachers included in this book were nominated by other educators as being exemplary computer-using teachers. Many have won awards and received national recognition for their exemplary teaching or for their innovative applications of technology.

Here is a sampling of what they have to say about the impact of computing in their lives:

> *As a high school English teacher and "technophobe," I decided to learn to use the dreaded computer. My hard-won ability to do so gave me such a thrill that I designed a computer-based writing course for "at risk" high school students. Their thrill of success was my impetus to integrate computers as the core of a brand-new creative writing magnet program.*
>
> —Michelle Starrett, Miami, Florida

> *Using the computer builds the self-concept of students in a variety of ways. The very idea that they are using a machine usually reserved for upper level students gives them something to be proud of and to brag about to their peers.*
>
> —Sharon Hurwitz, Norfolk, Virginia

> *I have initiated and implemented a comprehensive program that introduced computer skills to an elementary parochial school. As the children progressed through the program, they developed basic skills in keyboarding, word processing, and databases. Students at all levels were provided with software to encourage higher level thinking skills beyond drill and practice.*
>
> —Toni Votava, South Bend, Indiana

> *I had a dramatic career change because of computers. I was so excited that I quit my job and opened a computer learning center in order to create the type of learning environment that I felt computers permitted. I used the independent aspect of computer learning to mix ages and levels and to encourage a focus on students' own efforts.*
>
> —Jean Dames, Highland Park, Illinois

> *During the past two years I have been using a computer with home- and hospital-bound students. The computer is invaluable as a motivational and therapeutic tool when instructing confined children and youth. Students are able to see computer applications across the curriculum—integrated learning.*
>
> —Linda Copper, Baltimore, Maryland

Read on to find out what these and other teachers have to say about using computers in their classrooms!

Why Read This Book?

For anyone who cares about reform of education or the role of technology in Information Age schooling, this book should be interesting and enjoyable. Reading this book will give you an appreciation of the creativity of teachers. You will see some of the ways that teachers can take control of technology to make it support their own vision of learning and teaching. The book illustrates how technology can be used to make teaching more interesting and effective.

We hope that in the process of reading this book you will come to understand how computers can unlock your full potential as a teacher. If you become inspired, you will likely pass this inspiration on to your students and colleagues. Not only will you get more satisfaction from your own teaching but the quality of education in your school can be improved. Just think what a difference this could make to our overall school system.

Further Information

Most education computing textbooks do a good job describing past research in the field from a learning or student perspective (see the references in Chapter 14). However, there are relatively few sources that examine technology from a teacher perspective. Here are some recent studies:

Dwyer, D., Ringstaff, C. & Sandholtz, J. (April 1990). *The Evolution of Teachers' Instructional Beliefs and Practices in High Access to Technology Classrooms.* AERA Conference Proceedings, Boston, MA. [An Apple Computer ACOT Project Report]

Educational Technology 29, 3 (March 1989). Special issue on teacher training for technology.

Sheingold, K., & Hadley, M. (1990). *Accomplished Teachers: Integrating Computers into Classroom Practice.* Center for Technology in Education, Bank Street College of Education, New York, NY.

Wiske, M., et al. (March 1988). *How Technology Affects Teaching.* Technical Report 87-10. Educational Technology Center, Harvard Graduate School of Education, Cambridge, MA.

There is a large literature that describes what teachers do in the classroom. We consider this work to be fundamental to understanding how teachers can use technology in schools. Here are some key readings:

Jackson, P. W. (1968). *Life in Classrooms.* New York: Holt, Rinehart & Winston.

Johnson, S.M. (1990). *Teachers at Work.* New York: Basic Books.

Kidder, T. (1989). *Among Schoolchildren.* Boston: Houghton Mifflin.

Kohl, H. (1984). *Growing Minds: On Becoming a Teacher.* New York: Harper & Row.

Lortie, D. C. (1975). *Schoolteacher: A Sociological Study.* Chicago: University of Chicago Press.

Books that discuss the history of educational technology contain important lessons and insights for teachers and administrators to consider. Here are three excellent ones:

Cuban, L. (1986). *Teachers and Machines: The Classroom Use of Technology Since 1970.* New York: Teachers College Press.

Gagne, R. (1986). *Instructional Technology: Foundations.* Hillsdale, NJ: Erlbaum Assoc.

Saettler, P. (1990). *The Evolution of American Educational Technology.* Littleton, CO: Libraries Unlimited.

Activities

• Informally survey 5-10 teachers at a school. Ask them why they use/don't use computers in their teaching. What are the factors that seem to determine whether or not computers are used?

• Ask students of different age groups what they think about using computers in school. What view of technology do their answers reflect?

• The history of technology in U.S. schools is not a very successful one (see the books by Cuban or Saettler listed above). Is there any reason to believe the new philosophy outlined in this chapter will lead to better results?

• Do you think the use of technology in the classroom has changed the traditional roles and activities of teachers? Will it change these roles and activities in the future?

• Make a timeline chart for the evolution of educational computing starting in 1960. You will have to decide which events are critical enough to include on your chart.

Chapter 2
Teacher Productivity

Teachers often complain that so much of their time is taken up with administrative chores that little time is left for actual teaching. Of course, many of these administrative duties are part of the teaching process: making up and scoring tests, keeping grades and attendance records, sending letters to parents, and completing paperwork on students. On the other hand, tasks such as keeping track of supplies, filling in budgets, attending school meetings, and supervising study hall or lunch periods may not seem worthwhile from a teaching perspective.

Computers can help teachers handle many of their administrative chores more efficiently and allow them to be more productive. In this chapter we examine how.

Making Schools More Efficient

> *The schools are slumbering under so much inefficiency, it keeps us from being effective in teaching and learning.*
>
> —Jennell Leonard

In her role as director of the Computer Training Laboratory for the Washington, D.C. schools, Jennell Leonard is responsible for training all instructional personnel—8,000 teachers, principals, assistant superintendents, directors, coordinators, clerical staff—at 200 locations. With her goal of improving the efficiency of the schools, Jennell begins by working with the principals. She finds that principals are concerned about the efficiency of their schools, but first they need to learn how technology can support what *they* do. Then they can move to a concern for the efficiency of their teachers. Jennell finds that by working with both teachers and principals, she can show them how to work together on making the *school* more effective. While she provides training to help them understand the capabilities of the technology, she tells both principals and teachers that *they* have the responsibility to decide how to use the technology to support what *they* know how to do.

> *What's still exciting to me is to look for the most efficient way to do a task, and choose an appropriate tool to accomplish it.*
>
> —Jennell Leonard

Creating and Scoring Tests

One of the perennial tasks of a teacher is to make up tests and keep grades. This is one task that computers can make much easier. Consider the process of making up tests. One easy way to do this is to use a word processing program (see the next chapter for more about word processing). You type in your test questions in the exact form that you want and print them out. You can create a large set of test questions and only print out a subset for a particular quiz or exam.

One drawback to using a word processor to create tests is that you have to arrange the questions yourself. If you wanted to put the questions in a different order or format, you would need to move and copy text. This is where a test generation program can help. Test generation programs create the test for you once you have typed in your content and specified the format of the test (e.g., multiple choice, fill-in-the-blank, matching, etc.).

Some test generators will let you produce an online version of the test that students can take at the computer. When students take the test at the computer, the testing program scores their responses according to the answers you have provided. The test generator not only saves you time in creating the test but also saves you the trouble of scoring it as well. Both you and the students get the results as soon as they have completed the test.

Of course, online testing means that each student must have access to a computer to take the test and that you have a way to collate the scores from all the students. If they all use the same computer, or if all the computers used are part of a network, this will work well. Another alternative is to print the tests and have the students record their answers on a mark sense reader (MSR) or optical character reader (OCR) answer sheet. The MSR/OCR sheet can be decoded by a MSR/OCR device and the scores tabulated automatically. Most MSR/OCR devices are designed to work with test generation programs and vice-versa.

How much time can be saved? A lot. Once you have input your test content into a test generation program, the tests are immediately available for use. If you have the computer score the tests, scoring can be done as soon as the student is finished (in the case of online testing) or in a few minutes if you run the tests through an MSR/OCR device. Of course, automated test scoring does not work for essay/open answer responses so this could be a limiting factor if you use this kind of test.

Computers can also play an important role in developing new forms of student evaluation. For example, there is a widespread movement in the field of educational measurement to go beyond standard, multiple choice tests and develop measures that better represent instructional outcomes and enable students to demonstrate their skills directly. One major approach is assessment of student portfolios. Portfolios contain samples of students' writing or other products. A teacher or group of teachers, sometimes in conjunction with the students, develops a set of criteria for systematic evaluation of the portfolios. There is exciting potential for hypermedia portfolios in all subject areas. The range of materials that can be stored in hypermedia formats includes written samples (scanned if handwritten), art work (scanned if not computer generated), video, and audio.

A Week in the Life of an Information Age Teacher

Peter MacLeod is a geography teacher at Philemon Wright High School, in Hull, Quebec. When he completed this weekly journal he was (1) teaching two geography classes, (2) testing a program called *Telichart*, a graphics delivery system for data from Statistics Canada (a federal agency), (3) writing curriculum for Statistics Canada to assist in the teaching of population studies, and (4) involved in two telecommunications projects concerned with exchanging geographic information among schools in Canada and Italy. Here is a summary of Peter's computer activities during the week:

Monday

- Xerox broken, so printed a test on stencils and ran them off. Lucky to have a duplicate computer at home and school.
- Printed grade record sheet (McGuffey's Grader).

• Helped student use Telichart to look for crime statistics for a debate on family violence. Printed graph and data.
• In the evening, created a review sheet for midyear exams and wrote several letters (WordPerfect).

Tuesday

• Connected with Montreal to receive an electronic mail message from Italy and replied (Procomm).
• Printed and copied exam outlines for both courses. (One was created last year and only needed reediting).
• In the evening, graded tests and ran analysis of results (McGuffey's Grader).

Wednesday

• Reprinted grades and did end of term calculation; printed student reports with appropriate comments (McGuffey's Grader).
• Connected with Telichart for information on wheat and milk production in eastern and western Canada; printed graphs and made transparencies for class.
• Made crossword puzzles to help students review for midyear exams (Crossword Magic).
• Wrote memo to Statistics Canada about an upcoming meeting (WordPerfect) and then sent it via fax.
• In evening, made worksheets from old exams by cutting and pasting (WordPerfect).

Thursday

• Used desktop publishing program to create a notice for teachers to see Telichart in action (Publish It!).
• Created banners for new wall displays as part of an effort to redecorate the classroom (Print Shop).
• Printed information about the Dominican Republic for a student planning to vacation there during the March break (PC Globe+).
• Used a database (First Choice) to prepare an order of films for next semester, printed it, and sent it via fax.
• In evening, found an article on handheld scanners for a fellow teacher.

Friday

• Replied to a message from Italy concerning topics of discussion and holiday schedule for February-March.
• Demonstrated Telichart to a group of teachers

• Refined some old and created some new worksheets for next semester (WordPerfect).
• Finished student worksheets for Statistics Canada project (WordPerfect) and sent them via fax.

Keeping Grades and Attendance

Regardless of whether you take advantage of the computer to create and score tests, you can still use it for keeping track of grades. One of the simplest ways to do this is to use a spreadsheet set up with the students' names as the rows and each test or class activity as a column (for example, see Figure 2-1). You can write formulas to add the scores across the rows and columns as well as compute the means. This will give you a cumulative grade for each student as well as an idea of how all the students did on a given test or activity.

There are additional things you can do with this basic model. For example, you can write a formula that will display a list of all students who are below or above a certain grade level. You might need this list for creating parent letters or an honor roll. Instead of grades, you might record completion of objectives or instruction units in an individual education program (IEP). In this case, you would use 0s and 1s to indicate completion. Or you could create report cards for individual students by combining their grades from separate spreadsheets for each subject.

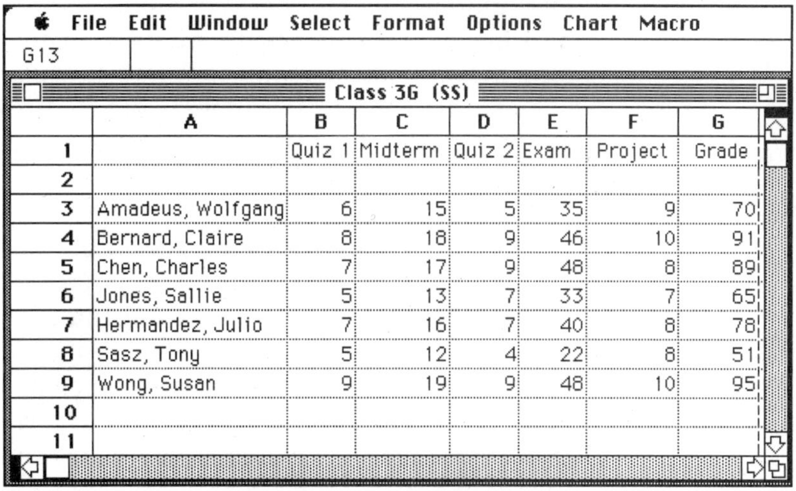

	A	B	C	D	E	F	G
1		Quiz 1	Midterm	Quiz 2	Exam	Project	Grade
2							
3	Amadeus, Wolfgang	6	15	5	35	9	70
4	Bernard, Claire	8	18	9	46	10	91
5	Chen, Charles	7	17	9	48	8	89
6	Jones, Sallie	5	13	7	33	7	65
7	Hermandez, Julio	7	16	7	40	8	78
8	Sasz, Tony	5	12	4	22	8	51
9	Wong, Susan	9	19	9	48	10	95
10							
11							

Figure 2-1 Sample spreadsheet for keeping grades

Spreadsheets work equally well for keeping track of attendance. Student names are listed as rows in the spreadsheet with days or class periods as columns. You indicate presence or absence using 0s and 1s in each cell of the spreadsheet. By computing the totals across the columns, you get the total times absent for each student. Computing the totals across the rows provides a picture of absences for given days or periods.

Instead of using spreadsheets for grading, IEPs, or attendance, you can buy programs specifically designed for this purpose. This saves you the time of making up your own format. On the other hand, the advantage of making up your own is that you can design it exactly as you want it. Another option is to use a spreadsheet template that someone else has designed. There are lots of these available on computer bulletin boards and in public domain software catalogs. Using a predesigned template saves you the time of making one from scratch but also allows you the flexibility to make changes if you want.

Integrated Packages and Templates

One category of software that you will hear a lot about are so-called "integrated packages." An integrated package is a combination of four or five applications program including word processing, spreadsheet, database, graphics and telecommunications, designed to work together smoothly. This means that you can move data from one program to another easily. It also means that you only need to learn or teach one interface (set of commands) for all the different programs. If you are using application software in the classroom, having to deal with only one program instead of four or five makes life a lot simpler!

AppleWorks and Microsoft *Works* are the most common integrated packages found in schools. In higher education and the business world, Lotus 1-2-3 and Microsoft Excel are very popular.

Another valuable aspect of using integrated packages is the availability of hundreds of templates for specific applications. A template is a predefined worksheet for a specific application such as an annual budget or a lesson plan. These templates are typically available at nominal cost. For example, Heizer publishes a catalog of templates for Excel and Works and K-12 MicroMedia Publishing distributes templates for AppleWorks. There are a number of AppleWorks and Works workbook/disk packages available for teachers (see Further Information). Also worth knowing about is *Microsoft Works in Education*, a quarterly newsletter published by the ISTE.

Parent Letters

Another time-consuming activity for most teachers is writing letters to parents telling them about the progress of their children or inviting them to a conference. In fact, this is such a tedious activity that many teachers do the minimal amount necessary. Word processing and a capability called "mail merge" can change all that.

Mail merge works as follows. First you create a master copy of the letter you want to send with the variable information such as names and addresses, grades, or dates indicated by special markers. Next you create a separate file containing all the variable information. Then have the computer print the letters by filling in the variable information in each letter from the list in the file. While you're at it, you can also have the computer print mailing labels for the envelopes from the same file.

Next time you want to send a set of letters to parents, you make any changes necessary to the master copy and the variable information list, and print them out. Once you have taken the time to create the information list, you can reuse it with as many different kinds of letters or forms that you wish.

Most word processing programs come with a mail merge capability either built in the program or as a separate utility. Labels can be created by arranging names and addresses in three columns across the page and printing them on special label stock.

The Educator HomeCard

The Educator HomeCard (EHC) is a set of stacks developed for use with HyperCard 2.0 (see chapter 10 for more about HyperCard). The EHC contains a variety of useful teacher's tools including a seating chart, a gradebook, a student information database, a daily planner, a presentation program, and other teacher resources (see Figure 2-2). It also includes a collection of clip art and sample lessons.

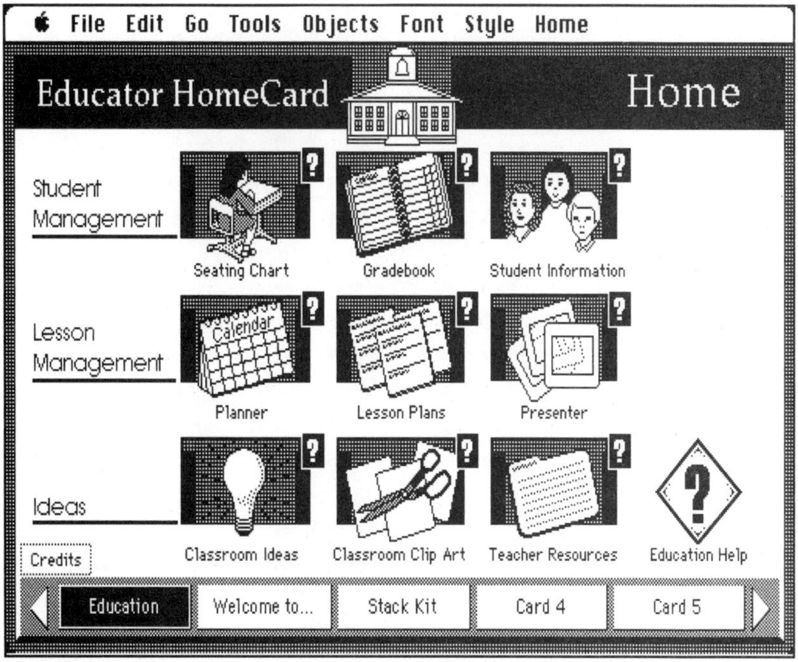

Figure 2-2 Educator HomeCard (Apple Computer, Inc.)

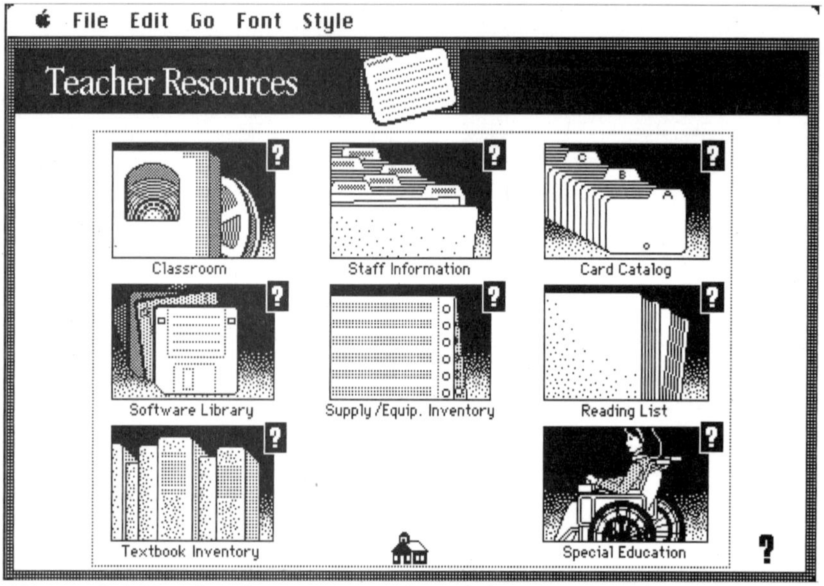

Figure 2-3 Teacher Resources section of the EHC (Apple Computer, Inc.)

The Teacher Resources section of the EHC (see Figure 2-3) contains predefined templates for creating a card catalog, software library, inventories, reading lists, and IEPs for special education students. Although the functions that the EHC provides are not sophisticated, they will probably meet the needs of most teachers and can always be modified by anyone who knows how to write with HyperCard.

The Educator Home-Card is distributed by Intellimation.

Keeping Track of Things

Another chore that often falls to teachers is keeping track of students (e.g., who has what books, parent phone numbers, etc.) or school supplies and equipment. For example, imagine that you are the school band director and you need to keep records about who has which instruments or uniforms. You could keep all the information on index cards or in a record book. If there are only a few students and you don't need to look up the information very often, then this method will work. However, if there are a lot of records and you need to answer questions frequently, a computer database will probably be helpful and save time.

When you use a database program, you start by defining the fields of information that you want to keep. This would include names, addresses, telephone numbers, equipment descriptions or serial numbers, dates, value, or locations. Once you have defined the fields, you enter the information into a separate record for each student or entity in your database. As you get new information or when information changes you can add or modify the records in the database. Figure 2-4 shows an example.

After you have put information in a database, you can do a number of things with it. You can search through the database to find records that contain specific information. For example, you could identify all the stu-

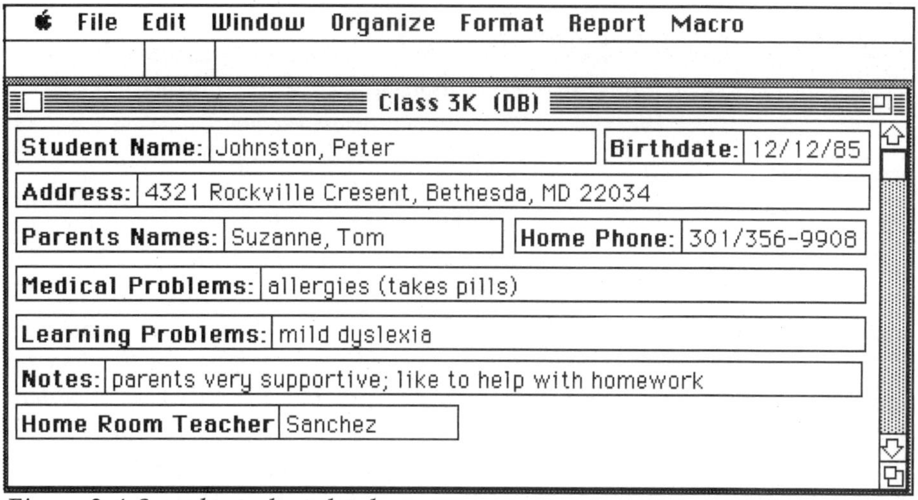

Figure 2-4 Sample student database.

dents who play trumpet or which student owns an instrument with a specific serial number. You can print reports that contain only the fields you are interested in rather than all the information in the database. Databases also allow you to sort information in whatever order you specify. So, if you want to make a list of all uniforms according to date of purchase or by size, you would be able to do this easily.

There are many database programs to choose from. They vary in their capabilities and ease of use. As a general rule, the easier a program is to learn, the less capability it has. If you are looking for a program to do small databases (e.g., no more than 1,000 records), you should have no trouble finding one that is inexpensive and can be learned quickly. On the other hand, if you are planning to create a large database (i.e., thousands or millions of records), you will need a more powerful program that may take longer to learn. You can also buy special purpose database programs that are already set up for certain kinds of record keeping, which saves you the trouble of designing the database yourself.

From Grade-books to Networks

Russ Doren is a science teacher at Cherry Creek High School in Colorado. He explains how the Macintosh has come to be a critical productivity tool in his teaching:

> *On a regular basis, I use many Mac programs to make my job easier. I use Microsoft Excel for my gradebook and use MacWrite, WriteNow, or Microsoft Works for word processing. I use SuperPaint 2.0 for graphics with clip art packages, Crossword Magic for crossword puzzles, and CalendarMaker, just to name a few. If I am not grading papers during planning periods, I can usually be found upgrading my gradebook, fixing overheads, rewriting labs, making crossword puzzles, or helping troubleshoot for my colleagues.*

One very popular use of technology has been using the Mac to produce overheads and lab sheets. My colleagues and I are always in the process of changing our overheads and producing them on the Mac. We have developed literally hundreds of overheads the last few years based on Macintosh technology, as opposed to handwritten overheads of the past. The copy for the overheads is easy to modify and is always printed neatly for the students to use. We also are in the process of converting many of our lab sheets to Macintosh technology for the same reasons.

Another effort my colleagues and I have undertaken is to establish a database test bank of biology test questions. During the last two years, we have used the program MicroTest III and have typed all of our unit exams and final exams into our test bank. We can now generate laser-printed multiple version exams for all of our tests. We are going to be switching textbooks in the next couple of years and will be adding a great number of questions to our test bank. Right now our test bank contains about 700 questions. We enjoy the flexibility and ease of use of the computer to help us with our exams and can generate new exams with very short notice.

Another responsibility I have taken on is science department Macintosh Network Administrator. For the past two years, I have taken classes on how to help administer and troubleshoot a Macintosh network. Last year, our library purchased one Mac for each department and a Mac IIx with 140 megabyte hard drive. In mid-April the Macintoshes were distributed to all of the departments (in four different buildings) and a true computer network was established, including E-mail. Our networked software includes numerous clipart packages, Microsoft Works, HyperCard, and Microsoft PowerPoint. I have really enjoyed helping all of our department's Mac enthusiasts become computer literate on using software through a true computer network.

Linking to Other Systems

Most large school systems today have some form of centralized data processing system that provides word processing, spreadsheet, and database capabilities. However, these capabilities often are not available to teachers or even individual school administrators. Many large schools have created their own networks that link a number of computers in the school. Such networks are typically used for the processing of administrative data including grades, test results, attendance, and personnel records. Like the larger data processing systems at the district level, these school-based networks also have word processing, spreadsheet, and database capabilities.

Since teachers are often required to provide input of grades, reports, and records to these systems, the question of transferring data from one computer to another often arises. Suppose you use a spreadsheet to keep grades for your classes on your own personal computer and you want to transfer these grades to the computer system used by the office for generating report cards. If you are lucky, the office computer system will be compatible with your computer and you can hand over a floppy disk containing the grade file. If the systems aren't compatible, you can still transfer the file via a telecommunications link.

The direction of information flow can go the other way, too. There may be data or programs on the district system that you would like to transfer to your personal computer or just be able to access at certain times. For example, imagine that you could connect with the master student record system and obtain the work telephone number of a student's parent. Or your school system may have test item or lesson plan databases that you can access.

While we're on the subject of telecommunications and linking to other systems, there is one other important type of computer network we should mention—networks that have been specifically designed to link teachers and schools together. There are a number of these, but the largest and most ambitious is called PSINet (People Sharing Information Network), part of the Mastery in Learning Project sponsored by the National Education Association. PSINet, which connects hundred of schools around the country, allows teachers to share ideas, experiences, and advice with each other. The goal of the project is help teachers discover new ways of teaching and ultimately to cause a restructuring of the education system.

In Chapter 5 we will discuss the use of electronic networks in more detail. At this point we want to introduce the idea of linking with other computers to transfer or share data.

The Compatibility Nightmare

One of the big nuisance factors of using computers is incompatibility—when one hardware or software component doesn't work with another.

The most common incompatible components are floppy disks. There are different formats for storing data on disks and every type of computer uses a different format. This means that Apple computers cannot read the disks created by IBM computers and vice-versa. Even worse, because of their different densities, a disk created on one computer may not be usable on another computer, even though it is the same brand.

Programs and files can be incompatible as well. A text file created by one word processing program cannot be loaded by a different word processing program (unless special precautions are taken to save it in a "plain" text format). A graphics file created by a graphics editor may not load into a program that is supposed to accept graphics. Worse yet, a file created by one version of a program may not work with a newer or older version of the same program.

Similarly, some programs can only work with newer or older versions of an operating system or hardware. For example, IBM PCs have a number of different types of graphics standards. A program designed to use EGA or VGA graphics will not run on older PCs that only support CGA graphics. Compatibility problems can be caused by memory limitations. Newer programs tend to require a lot more memory than older programs and hence many will not run on older computers.

There are also many types of compatibility problems associated with printers. Typically a program will work with certain printers but not others. More commonly, a program will work with a given printer, but not be able to do all the printing functions that the printer or software is capable of performing.

A lot of time can be wasted trying to solve or understand a compatibility problem. There is only one real antidote to incompatibility woes: Make sure something works on your system before you buy it!

Summary

In this chapter we examined the idea of computers as administrative assistants that can help reduce the amount of time spent on routine chores such as grading, creating and scoring tests, keeping attendance, writing letters to parents, or keeping records. We discussed three types of software: spreadsheet, word processing, and database programs. We also mentioned the tradeoffs between making your own programs versus buying ready-made programs as well as the possibility of transfering data between computer systems.

There is a hidden agenda for becoming proficient with word processing, spreadsheets, and database programs. Once you understand how to improve your own personal productivity using these programs, you will start to see how they can be used in teaching activities as well. For example, if you use word processing to write parent letters, why not have students do the same? If you use spreadsheets for grades, how about students using them for math problems or science data? Or how about using databases for organizing history or geography facts?

As mundane as the applications discussed in this chapter may seem, they provide a good foundation for the use of computers in education. Chances are that once you start to use spreadsheet, word processing, and database software, you will say what most regular computer users say: "I can't imagine how I ever did this job without a computer!"

Further Information

There are a number of books focus on the use of application software in the classroom. Although these books are concerned with classroom activities, they may give you ideas for personal use:

Cannings, T., & Finkel, LeRoy. (1992). *The Technology Age Classroom: Using Technology as a Tool.* Wilsonville, OR: Franklin, Beedle & Associates.

Collis, B. (1988). *Computers, Curriculum, and Whole Class Instruction: Issues and Ideas.* Belmont, CA: Wadsworth.

Tuner, D., & Land, M. (1988). *Tools for Schools: Applications Software for the Classroom.* Belmont, CA: Wadsworth.

Here are some workbook/disk packages for AppleWorks or Works:

Finkel, L., McManus, J., & Zeitz, L. (1989). *Microsoft Works through Applications.* Gilroy, CA: Computer Literacy Press.

Luehrmann, A. & Peckam, H. (1986). *Hands-On AppleWorks.* Gilroy, CA: Computer Literacy Press.

Microsoft Corp. (1989). *In and Out of the Classroom with Microsoft Works.* Redmond, WA: Microsoft Press.

Nogales, P., & McAllister, C. (1987). *AppleWorks for Teachers.* Wilsonville, OR: Franklin, Beedle & Associates.

If you want to learn more about the administrative use of computers, here are some books you can investigate:

Bluhm, H. (1987). *Administrative Uses of Computers in the Schools.* Englewood Cliffs, NJ: Prentice-Hall.

Kearsley, G. (1990). *Computers for Educational Administrators: Leadership in the Information Age.* Norwood, NJ: Ablex.

Miller, H. (1988). *An Administrators Manual for the Use of Microcomputers in the Schools.* Englewood Cliffs, NJ: Prentice-Hall.

The addresses of the ISTE and the software companies mentioned in this chapter are provided in Chapter 14.

Activities

• See if you can find a test generation program and try it out. What advantages and disadvantages does it have over the use of a word processing program?

• Try to locate an OCR/MSR that you can use. Use it to score your next test. How well did it work? What are the advantages and disadvantages of scoring tests this way?

• Use a spreadsheet to create a grading or attendance sheet for your classes. Does it save time over manual methods? What are the strengths and limitations of using spreadsheets?

• Use a database program to create a student database for your students. You can turn this into a class activity by having the students input their own information and then conduct searches or generate reports.

• Use a word processing program with mail merge capability to create a set of letters to parents. What are advantages and disadvantages of using the mail merge capability?

• Obtain a template that someone else has created and try it out. What modifications would you make to the template? Try making these changes.

Chapter 3
Writing Better Electronically

One area in education that is undergoing dramatic change is writing. Computers are playing a major role in this change. Learning to write has often been a major frustration for students and teachers but with the advent of word processing, it becomes much easier. Teachers and students are using computers in many ways both to support the writing process and to expand their repertoire of published materials. Communication skills, including writing, are critical in all subjects. Beyond school, writing skills determine the kinds of jobs open to students and their career growth. For this reason, the impact of computers on writing is likely to be far reaching.

Word processing technology makes it possible for teachers and students to find real audiences for their work. At the same time, computers support the process approach to writing instruction, which emphasizes several different stages: prewriting (generating and collecting ideas), creating a draft (organizing and stating ideas), and revision (polishing the draft). The process writing approach stresses the importance of meaningful assignments (writing for real audiences) and peer collaboration/interaction.

Technology is also sparking a stronger interest by teachers and students in "writing across the curriculum." Writing and communicating ideas to audiences is no longer the sole province of the English or writing teacher. Indeed, writing is not only "across" the curriculum, but also "beyond" the curriculum. Consider the example of Peter Mazzocchi, a counselor at a junior high school. He spends a lot of time with students outside the classroom, and has observed that the children have many important concerns that are not addressed in the formal curriculum—concerns about divorce and family breakup, sex, drugs, teenage suicide, teenage runaways. He combined his personal interest in computers with his concern for the children by organizing a schoolwide project in which students produce a school magazine.

The students select topics of concern to them. Peter helps them find information and other resources such as people to interview. The students write the articles on these socially significant issues. Peter finds that the students become motivated not only to write, but to read as well. They even read the manuals for the desktop publishing software! But the most important outcomes are the students' realization through these published articles that they are not alone in their worries, and the adults' recognition of the legitimacy of the children's interests. Peter says, "The kids are egocentric, but we can give them a structure and a legitimate form for expression and communication with each other and their community."

Word processing software is the key element in the use of computers for writing activities at all ages. For younger students, drawing programs also play an important role. Tutorial, drill, and game software may be worthwhile for elementary and middle school students. At the high school and college level, writing utility programs are likely to be helpful. We will discuss and describe these different kinds of computer tools in this chapter.

Sometimes a Drawing Program is the Best Writing Software

For young children there is a close link between writing and drawing activities. Sonia Katzer, a kindergarten teacher at Louisville Elementary School in Louisville, Colorado explains:

> *In kindergarten, kids are still doing most of their writing through their drawing. So we start them drawing with MacPaint. Once the children are comfortable using the mouse for drawing, they use the text creation function of MacPaint for the initial writing steps. This may involve labeling pictures with beginning sounds or using different aspects of creative spelling.*

As the children move into first grade, they begin to use the word processing program *MacWrite* to compose more elaborate stories. They learn to use the clipboard to cut and paste their pictures from *MacPaint* to *MacWrite*. First grade teacher Chris Crnkovich comments:

> *Some compose at the computer. Others compose at their seats. They come to the computer to copy what they've written, and then expand, revise, and edit it. They've learned that writing has a purpose, that it's communication with another person or an audience. So they write to pen pals, and they write real books that go into the school library.*

By having students start with drawing pictures and then adding words to explain the pictures, these teachers introduce young children to writing as story-telling. So they learn writing in a meaningful context; the computer is simply a way to make it easier and more fun.

Source: *Writing Curriculum Guide*, Apple Computer.

Word Processing

Word processing programs come in all shapes and sizes. Some are designed for professional writers and include many sophisticated features. Others are designed for children or letterwriters and have minimal capabilities. As a general rule the more features a program has, the longer it takes to learn how to use.

All word processing programs contain a basic set of capabilities. Probably the most important feature of word processing is the ability to make as many changes to a document as desired before printing it. This includes adding and erasing characters, sentences, and paragraphs. Another important feature is the capability to copy or move text from one place to another. This capability is often called "cut and paste" from the old days of cutting things out and pasting them in another place. With some programs you can not only cut and paste text from one document to another, but you can also copy and move graphics or data.

Other important features of word processing programs include pagination (automatically organizing text into numbered pages), margin and tab settings, line spacing, and search/replace. Most word processing programs today also have advanced functions such as automatic footnoting, page headers and footers, hyphenation, and indexing. Many of the leading word processing programs now include desktop publishing capabilities as well (e.g., column layout, page previews). Desktop publishing is discussed in the next chapter.

Using Word Processing in the Classroom

The following writing activities illustrate the use of word processing in different settings. These activities can be done by individuals or small groups.

• Have students collect and analyze the selling techniques used in newspaper/magazine ads, such as repetition, testimonials, emotional appeals, status quo, and so on. Then have students write an ad for an imaginary product using these techniques.

• Have the students read a historical or geographical account and imagine that they are part of the story. Students should write diaries that describe their daily events. You can stimulate their imagination by showing films/videos that relate to the story and holding discussion groups about specific issues involved.

• Ask your students to write their family history describing each of their family members and ancestors. Have them create charts to show the family tree.

• Teach the students about different forms of poetry (limericks, shape poems, cinquains, haikus, etc.) and have each student write one or more types of poems. The poems can be collected and published in a book.

• Let students write their own adventure or interactive fiction stories. They will need to make outlines that show all the decision points and possible paths. Have the students program their stories using an programming language or authoring system (see chapter 10).

• Ask students to write a script for their favorite television program. They will need to identify the characters and work out a plot and dialogue for the episode. As an added twist, have the students act some of the episodes and videotape it!

Lesson Plans

Teachers have to do a lot of writing, including letters to parents, student reports, proposals, and lesson plans. Let's focus on this last category of documents to see how computers can help teachers with their writing chores.

Most teachers prepare a lesson plan for each class they teach (many states require it). Lesson plans usually involve the following elements: lesson objectives, preparation steps, resources required, student evaluation, and a description of the teaching/learning activities. Teachers can use word processing to prepare lesson plans in a number of ways. The job is made a little easier by preparing a master document with all the headings and filling it in for each lesson. Since there is often repetition in some elements of the plan, the ability to copy information from one plan to another (i.e., "cut and paste") is another time saver. The capability to easily revise a previously written plan is very important since there are always changes to be made.

Everything we have said about the use of word processing for lesson plans applies to all other types of writing activities. Word processing programs have many additional capabilities that can save time and effort. For example, in the previous chapter we discussed the value of mail merge in writing letters to parents. Although the use of word processing does not eliminate the work required to write something, it does make the process easier in many ways.

Incidentally, the Educator HomeCard for the Apple Macintosh (discussed in the previous chapter) includes a lesson plan stack designed to make lesson plan creation and organization even easier.

Putting the Meaning Back into Writing

El Cerrito High School is located just north of Berkeley, California. The students come mostly from the lower income industrial area of Richmond and the student population is predominantly black. Joan Cone, an English teacher at El Cerrito, explains the significance of computers to the students in this school:

> *At the beginning of the school year when we ask students what books they have read, they answer, "Books? We don't read books." And they are serious. The reading they have done in school has been piecemeal—parts of books their teachers have read aloud or passages from books transferred to worksheets. Any reading their teachers might assign for homework, they simply don't do. In writing, students have the same difficulties. They haven't done much of it. What they have done is in response to teacher assignments, and the only audience they write for is the teacher. Revision is an alien concept. "Revise? Do you mean I gotta copy it over?" they wail. They are rarely asked to use writing as a thinking tool, trying out ideas, changing their minds as they work through the messy process of drafting their writing. Instead, if they write at all, they often get stuck erasing misspelled words or misplaced punctuation—the surface features of their writing.*

However, word processing facilitates revising, proofreading (with spell checkers), student collaboration ("Try it this way—No, try it that way—I guess the first way was better"), and following through to a finished, computer-printed product. As one student said about his research paper last year, "Man, it even looks good." There is prestige in knowing how to use sophisticated technology and the added pride the use of computers produces in a student cannot be underestimated. Our experience has shown us that computers can play a vital role in fostering positive self-images through self-directed learning.

When students use the computer for writing, they tend to focus on what they are writing instead of the mechanics of the writing process. Ironically, the use of technology puts the focus back on writing to communicate in a way that most students miss when confronted with printed books or pen and paper. Maybe these results are not so strange when we think about computers as communication rather than calculating tools.

Student Writing

There are lots of reasons why students do poorly in writing. They get hung up in the details of spelling and grammar or finding the "right" words for a sentence. They may have difficulty expressing their ideas because of their limited vocabularies. Poor handwriting can make their efforts illegible and difficult to read. In many cases, students have low self-esteem and believe they have nothing to say that anyone else would care about reading.

Teachers use computers to help kids get over many of these hurdles. Word processing makes it easy to get ideas down and revise things. Gone is the tedious erasing and recopying. Online spelling checkers and thesauruses can be used by students to correct and expand their vocabulary. All writing can be legible and look good when printed.

Furthermore, word processing activities shift the focus of learning from lower-order skills such as memorization of vocabulary and grammar rules to the higher-order thinking skills involved in communication and problem solving. With word processing, students spend more time thinking about how to express their ideas and revising what they have written.

The beauty of word processing is that you can use the same program in almost any subject area. Students can write their assignments or projects in current events, science, history, health, or business classes. If you teach more than one subject or grade, you will be able to use word processing with different classes.

Using electronic mail and participating in online conferences facilitates the writing process even more. When students send messages to other students over a network, they are focusing on writing to communicate ideas or personal experiences. This makes writing activities interesting and meaningful in ways that a typical assignment is not. Even students who are reluctant to write may be drawn into electronic communications to share a common interest with other students. We discuss electronic communications further in Chapter 5.

The use of word processing leads naturally to desktop publishing activities. Producing a class newspaper or project report are usually very motivating events for students. They also foster teamwork and cooperation since students typically work in small groups for such activities. Desktop publishing is discussed in more detail in the next chapter.

Learning Critical Writing Skills via a Network

Deming High School serves a predominantly rural community in New Mexico. About 60 percent of the student population is Hispanic. Because of language difficulties, most of the students in Ken Leupold's English classes are below their grade levels in reading and writing skills. Ken describes how the use of a computer network has helped students improve their writing skills:

> *Students use BreadNet, the computer conferencing system developed by the Bread Loaf School of English in Vermont, to share their writing with schools in other parts of the country and world. This ability to share their writing is very important to these students because it gives them an audience other than the teacher to write for. At this time, students in one of my classes are exchanging writing with the American School in Peru and another class is sending its work to students in South Carolina. These classes exchange interviews or autobiographies, descriptions of their towns and schools, and ideas on subjects they wish to write about. They can be more free with their writing since they do not know the people to whom they are writing.*
>
> *We have also set up conferences for writing on BreadNet. One is called WORKSHOP. In this conference, each of a dozen schools puts up samples of creative writing, which are then critiqued by students from other schools. This allows the students to view the writing of others from a different vantage point. The students might feel uncomfortable at first critiquing a friend's work, but it is easy to talk to somebody they will never see about their writing. This ability to tell what is good from what needs work in writing eventually carries over into my classroom so they can help each other with their writing without feeling that they will lose a friendship for saying that something needs to be improved in a rough draft.*

In this example, reading and writing skills are improved through the use of a network. The network also provides a means of getting students to review one another's work in a nonthreatening way.

Typing Skills

Many teachers think it is a good idea to provide students with some basic keyboarding practice before they start word processing activities. Although lack of typing ability does not prevent kids from using word processing (lots of regular computer users are "two-finger typists"), the more typing ability they have, the faster they will be able to get things done. There are many typing practice programs available, many of which take the form of games that make learning to type interesting and fun. In fact, starting off with one of these games may be a good way to introduce your students to computers. Many elementary teachers use introduction to the keyboard as a opportunity to provide practice with the alphabet and numbers.

Writing Utilities

Many programs are available to help you and your students analyze their writing efforts. Most of these programs (often called style or grammar checkers) identify errors in grammar or punctuation. For example, they will detect "affect" instead of "effect," "to" instead of "too," mismatches between nouns and verbs, and many other common mistakes. The programs will also provide a measure of readability as well as critiques of writing style.

Some of these writing utilities can be useful in grading student work. They indicate the number of words per sentence or paragraph, the number of grammar mistakes made, or summarize repeated errors. A few programs will produce a report for the student that explains the errors made. Such programs do not take care of the whole grading job, but they can speed it up and provide more detailed information to base a grade on. There are also programs that make it easier to provide comments about student papers (see the description of PROSE below).

There are many programs available to help young children write stories, poetry, or other forms of prose. Some programs provide collections of graphics that can be selected and arranged by the students along with text that they add. Other programs provide story beginnings and ideas to continue them.

Finally, programs called outline or idea processors are designed to help with prewriting activities. These programs help students create, capture, and organize ideas before they start to write. Some of these programs let students draw diagrams to help visualize the relationships among ideas.

PROSE—A Tool for Teacher/Student Dialog

One of the difficult parts of teaching writing is providing feedback to students on their work. PROSE is a collaborative writing program for the Macintosh that was developed at Cornell University and is distributed commercially by McGraw-Hill. Nancy Kaplan, one of the developers of the program at Cornell, describes PROSE:

Students don't learn about writing from books—or from papers covered in red ink. They learn by interacting and exchanging perspectives. This is the thinking that led us to author PROSE. We wanted PROSE to not only make the commenting more efficient for instructors, but also somehow to make it more fruitful—both for ourselves and students. Commenting is the most onerous, time-consuming job for instructors, yet it's the pivot point of what we do.

The first thing you notice about PROSE is that you can mark directly on a student's text. There's a special window for your comments. You can write whatever you want in your window, but you can't cross out or interfere with the student's text. The student has his or her work and you have yours. If you notice grammatical or stylistic errors, you can quickly point them out by inserting special markers—and even incorporate exercises dealing with the particular problem. Students can respond by revising their text or even by using a "Reply" feature to explain what they were trying to do. This increases the sense that there is a real dialog going on.

PROSE is designed to run on a network so anyone in a class could access anyone else's work. This means that the commenting doesn't always have to come from the teacher. Students can review each other's work and get a sense of belonging to a community of writers.

Source: *Writing Curriculum Guide*, Apple Computer

What About Reading?

Computers are also useful for teaching children how to read. There are many different kinds of programs available such as letter recognition games, spelling drills, word puzzle generators, and interactive stories.

One of the most popular programs in schools is *Reader Rabbit* (The Learning Company). The program uses a number of different game strategies to introduce young children (ages 3-7) to letters and words. It also features sound and animation that capture children's attention and interest. The program allows the vocabulary to be changed making it possible to customize the program to a specific lesson topic or activity.

Sunburst Communications markets adventure games that are based on outstanding children's books such as *Charlotte's Web* or *Island of the Blue Dolphins.* The programs can be used in conjunction with the books to strengthen vocabulary or increase comprehension. There are also videotapes and class activity materials available for these books.

Another interesting program is *Reading Realities* from Teacher Support Software. The reading selections provided in the program reflect the concerns actually expressed by students about school, family, and personal issues. Students select a topic, see a picture on the screen and try to predict what the story is about before actually reading the story. The program provides a sound option so students can hear the story read to them (if the appropriate hardware is available).

However, the program that undoubtedly has had the most impact on reading education is *Writing to Read,* developed by Henry Martin and marketed by IBM Corp. The program focuses on writing with word processors in conjunction with a phonemic spelling system. Although *Writing to Read* involves a number of noncomputer activities, the computer component is usually credited with the effectiveness of the program. And the program has been shown to be highly effective by many independent evaluation studies.

For summaries of the research and practice associated with computers and reading, see the books by Blanchard et al. (1987), Strickland, Feeley & Wepner (1987), or Reinking (1987).

Summary

The use of computers for writing activities is dramatically changing the nature of language arts and English classrooms. Word processing not only makes writing easier for most students but it allows them to concentrate on what they are writing about. It leads to an emphasis on meaningful assignments (writing for real audiences), encourages collaboration, and facilitates cross-disciplinary learning activities. Word processing also makes writing easier for teachers. The writing of lesson plans, parent letters, proposals, and reports can be done faster with better quality results.

In addition to word processing software, many other types of software can be useful in writing activities. Typing "tutors" can improve typing skills. Writing utilities such as spelling and grammar checkers, electronic thesauruses, and outline processors can all help improve writing skills. There are also many types of programs designed to improve reading abilities.

Further Information

As you can see from this chapter, computers can help you improve the writing skills of your students in many ways. The books by Bolter (1990), Costanzo (1989), Daiute (1985), Knapp (1986), and Wresch (1987) discuss the topic in much more detail. A book by Elder, Bowen, Schwartz, & Goswami (1989) describes the experiences of the Bread Loaf School using networks to facilitate writing. The National Council for Teachers of English (NCTE) also publishes a number of books that discuss the use of computers for writing.

Two journals, *The Writing Notebook* and *Computer Assisted Composition Journal* discuss the latest ideas and research in this area. An article by Wresch (1988) provides a good overview of the writing utility programs available. Marcus (1989-90) has written a series of articles about the use of HyperCard for writing activities.

Apple Computer has published a writing curriculum guide that provides case studies of schools using the Macintosh for writing. The National Project on Computers and College Writing has a published a book of profiles that describe how colleges around the country use computers for writing activities.

References

Apple Computer. (1990) *Writing Curriculum Guide.* Available from LIST Services, 10810 Harney St., Suite 202, Omaha, NE 68154. (402) 334-4991.

Blanchard, J. S., et al. (1987). *Computer Applications in Reading.* Newark, DE: International Reading Assoc. (302) 731-1600.

Bolter, J. (1990). *The Writing Space: The Computer and the History of Writing.* Hillsdale, NJ: Erlbaum.

Computer Assisted Composition Journal. Methodist College, Fayette, NC 28311-1499.

Constanzo, W. (1989). *The Electronic Text: Learning to Write, Read and Reason with Computers.* Englewood Cliffs, NJ: Educational Technology Publications.

Daiute, C. (1985). *Writing and Computers.* Reading, MA: Addison-Wesley.

Elder, J., Bowen, B., Schwartz, J., & Goswami, D. (1989). *Word Processing in a Community of Writers.* New York: Garland Publishing Co.

Knapp, L. (1986). *The Word Processor and the Writing Teacher.* Englewood Cliffs, NJ: Prentice-Hall.

Marcus, S. (Sept./Oct. 1989, Nov./Dec. 1989, Jan./Feb. 1990, Apr./May 1990). What are HyperCard? Parts I-IV. *The Writing Notebook.*

National Council for Teachers of English (NCTE), 1111 Kenyon Rd., Urbana, IL 61801. (217) 328-3870.

National Project on Computers and College Writing.(1989) *Computers and College Writing: Selected College Profiles.* New York: The Instructional Resource Center, City University of New York.

Reinking, D. (1987). *Reading and Computers: Issues for Theory and Practice.* New York: Teachers College Press.

Strickland, D. S., Feeley, J. T., & Wepner, S. B. (1987). *Using Computers in the Teaching of Reading.* New York: Teachers College Press.

Wresch, W. (1987). *Practical Guide to Computer Uses in the English-Language Arts Classroom.* Englewood Cliffs, NJ: Prentice-Hall.

Wresch, W. (April 1988). Six directions for computer analysis of writing. *The Computing Teacher*, p. 13.

The Writing Notebook: Creative Word Processing in the Classroom. P.O. Box 79, Mendocino, CA 95460. (707) 937-2848.

Activities

• Think of three different ways you could use computers for prewriting activities, i.e., to encourage ideas and help students get started.

• Think about all the writing activities you do as a teacher. Which one do you think could benefit most from word processing? Which one least?

• Make a list of concerns you might have when using computers to teach writing. How could these concerns be addressed?

• Obtain one or more writing tutorial, drill, or game programs to evaluate. What are their strengths and weaknesses?

• Obtain one or more writing utility programs and develop a lesson plan that involves the use of this software.

Chapter 4
Desktop Publishing

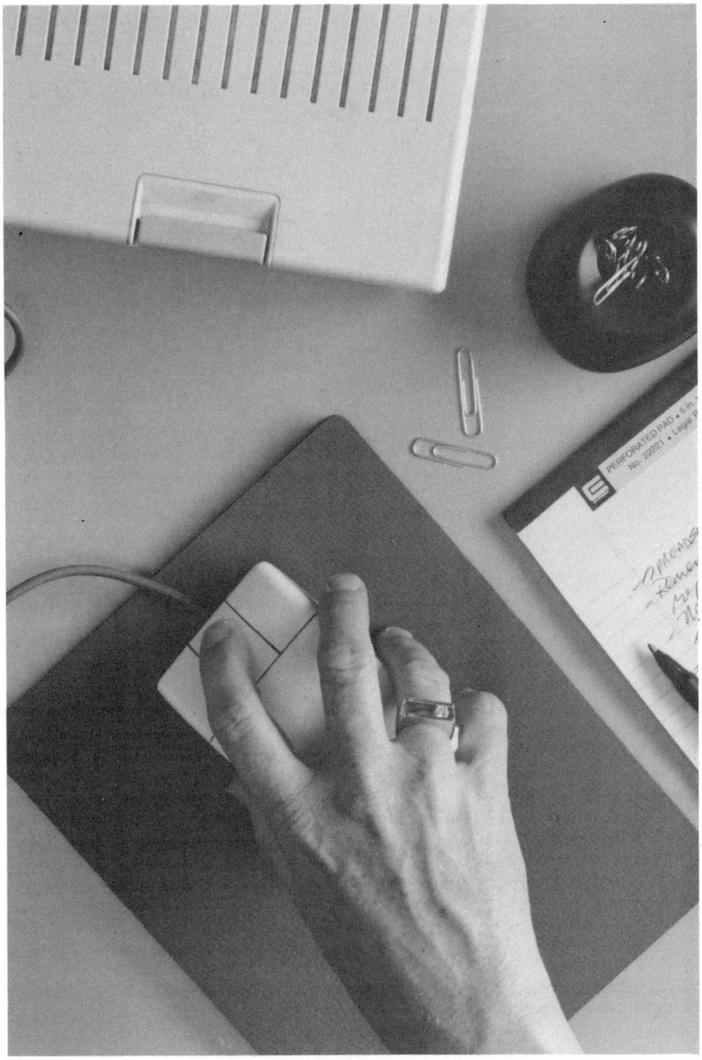

Next to writing activities and word processing applications, the second most popular use of computers in schools is probably for desktop publishing. Indeed, desktop publishing is closely related to writing and emerges naturally from word processing activities. Whereas word processing focuses attention on the process of writing and the content, desktop publishing concerns the way in which information is assembled and distributed.

Desktop publishing refers to the use of personal computers to produce professional-looking (i.e., printed) documents. The key elements of desktop publishing are page layout programs and laser printers. Page layout programs allow you to bring together text and graphics and organize them into pages. Laser printers produce high-quality printed output. In addition, a digitizer or scanner converts photographs and drawings to computer format. Desktop publishing makes it possible for students, teachers, and administrative staff to have access to their own electronic print shop.

Desktop Publishing Takes Over

Paul Matray is a biology teacher at the Robert Louis Stevenson School in Pebble Beach, California, an independent K-12 school with a student enrollment of 500. Here is his chronicle of how desktop publishing affected his school:

The school purchased a Macintosh system during the summer. I spent a few weeks familiarizing myself with the Macintosh and software during August. In September when the students returned, I sat down with the two layout editors of our student newspaper for about three hours and taught them what I had learned during the previous two weeks. In that these students were familiar with computers, they understood the basic operations and could quickly acquire the skills necessary to lay out the first issue of the paper four weeks later.

After the faculty at Stevenson saw the student newspaper, they realized there were other applications which could make their life less complicated. The athletic director asked me to prepare the program for the home football games and various sports posters. The music director asked me to prepare the programs for the winter and spring concerts. The drama department asked the layout editor of the newspaper to prepare the programs for the school plays. During the summer of 1989, I produced the College Counseling Guide, Student Handbook, Parent Guide, Prefect Guide, and Faculty Guide. I also produced two documents (laboratory manual, course reader) for my biology classes.

For educational institutions the application of this technology has far-reaching implications. It is a recent development and will become an integral part of most institutions over the next decade. It is an obvious choice because it saves money, teaches a skill which is readily marketable, and it can be used for our profession to take on a more professional air.

Source: IFIP Fifth World Conference on Computers in Education (WCCE) Proceedings (North-Holland, 1990).

Page Layout Software

Page layout (also called page composition) programs are designed to do what the name suggests—lay out pages by combining text and graphics. The text is usually created with a word processor and loaded into the page layout program from disk files. Graphics are normally created with a painting or drawing program (see Chapter 11) and also loaded from disk files. The page layout program lets you arrange the text into columns and position the graphics where desired. Furthermore, you can specify elements (such as a banner or logo) that occur on every page.

Let's look at a quick example to see how this works. Imagine that we are creating a simple two-page newsletter. Suppose that we have already written the articles using a word processor and saved them as text files. We have also used a drawing program to create a logo that we want to place on the first page beside the banner. First, we make up the banner with the space for the logo identified and indicate the location of the text columns using empty rectangles (see Figure 4-1).

Next, we load the logo into the appropriate space and load the text into the columns. The program automatically takes care of fitting the words into the space identified, "flowing" the words from one column to another. If the logo is too big or too small for the box we have specified, we can have the program change its size to fit the box (rescaling). Alternatively, we might only want to show part of the logo (this is called "cropping"). We could move the logo around in the box until we get exactly what we want. If we want to experiment with the location of the logo on the page, we can move it around using the mouse or arrow keys. When we are happy with the design of our newsletter, we can print it. Figure 4-2 shows the completed newsletter

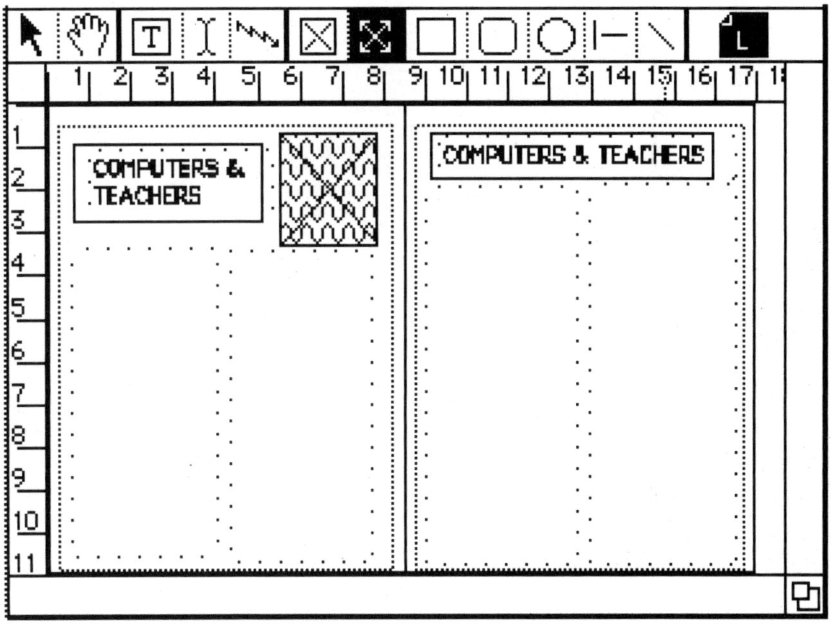

Figure 4-1 Creating a newsletter.

This example illustrates one of the important concepts of desktop publishing, WYSIWYG (pronounced "wisiwig") which stands for "what you see is what you get." This means that the way the document looks on the screen is the way it will look when printed. Before page layout software came along, it was not possible to see what the final document looked like on the screen.

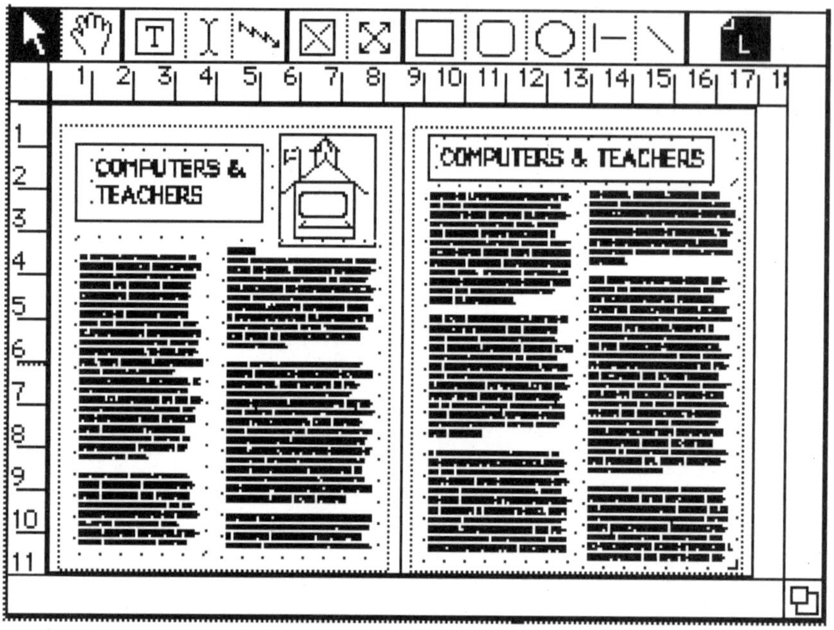

Figure 4-2 Completed newsletter.

The use of graphics software to create drawings and illustrations is an important aspect of desktop publishing. However, not everyone is an artist! This is where clip art comes in. Clip art refers to collections of illustrations that can be purchased in disk form and used for free. There are hundreds of clip art collections available and some desktop publishing programs include sets of clip art. Recently, publishers have started to distribute multimedia clip art on CD-ROM that includes photographs as well as illustrations.

Producing a School Newspaper

One of the best and most popular uses of desktop publishing is to produce a school newspaper. It's an activity that most students find interesting and one that can be linked to many aspects of the curriculum. Here are some of the steps involved:

- Have students analyze actual newspapers and become familiar with the various sections and the composition. Also introduce them to the various staff roles involved in publishing a newspaper. A field trip to a local newspaper office or a guest talk by a newspaper editor are good ideas.
- Students should select the role they want to play (e.g., writer, editor, photographer, production supervisor, advertising director, etc.). Have all writers decide what section they want to write for (e.g., news, sports, business, travel, entertainment, etc.). Encourage writers to conduct a personal interview with a person relevant to their "beat" and use this as the basis for their story.

• The writers should type up their "copy" and submit it to the editors for review/rewriting. Have photographers take or find photos to illustrate the stories.
• The students in charge of advertising should compose and develop ads for school activities or local businesses (this could be real). Students in charge of classified ads should solicit ads from the student body, teachers, staff, and parents.
• The editor-in-chief should be responsible for the arrangement or organization of the newspaper. The production supervisor determines the exact layout and assembly of the paper.
• Once the newspaper is completed, duplicate it and distribute it to the school/community.

Scanners and Digitizers

What happens when you want to include photographs in your desktop publishing documents? The answer is to use a scanner or digitizing camera. Scanners look like copying machines or laser printers except they work in reverse. Instead of producing printed documents, they produce an electronic version of the document that is scanned. You can save the scanned image (e.g., photograph, illustration, drawing) as a disk file and then load it into a desktop publishing program. You can also load the file into a graphics program and modify it if you wish.

Scanners come in many different shapes and sizes. There are hand-held scanners that you move across something you want to convert to electronic form. They are relatively inexpensive and useful for many desktop publishing projects. Most scanners only do black and white; color scanners are available but they are very expensive.

A digitizing camera performs the same function as a scanner but it stores an image of whatever the camera is focused upon. This allows you to point the camera at any object or scene and create a graphics file of the object or scene. Using a digitizing camera is a great way to capture "mug shots" of students and teachers for inclusion in school publications.

Scanners introduce an ethical problem that every teacher has to deal with in desktop publishing—copyright infringement. A scanner makes it easy to capture illustrations or photos from books and magazines for republishing in new documents. Students must be taught to always credit their sources and to request permission to use other people's work. Of course this is just one of the many copyright issues that comes with technology use. Other issues include the illegal copying of software or illegal access to online databases.

Laser Printers

The major hardware element of desktop publishing is the laser printer. Unlike dot matrix or ink jet printers, which rely on a moving head to do the printing, a laser printer "paints" the image on the paper in one pass. Because of the way they work, laser printers produce much more detail and are faster than other kinds of printers. A typical laser printer will have a resolution of 300 dpi (dots per inch) and a speed of 8 ppm (pages per minute). Another important characteristic of most laser printers is that they are designed to be used in a network so many computers can share them.

Note that you don't have to have a laser printer to do desktop publishing. However, if you want your publications to look really professional, a laser printer is necessary. Many schools use inexpensive dot matrix printers for the initial work and save the laser printer for the final printing.

Graphics Arts Skills

In addition to page layout software, scanners, and laser printers, there is one other element that is important in desktop publishing—graphics arts skill. Unless you know some of the basic principles of design of effective print documents, the results of your desktop publishing efforts may not be very readable or attractive.

Some standard guidelines include the following:

- Leave lots of "white space" in page layouts and avoid cramming too much into a single page.
- Break pages of text into two or three columns.
- Use headings and titles often.
- Use lines and boxes to organize pages.
- Avoid the use of too many different typefaces or type sizes.

Following the principles of graphics arts in desktop publishing is analogous to observing the rules of grammar in writing/word processing. The references at the end of this chapter include books that cover design principles for desktop publishing.

Desktop Publishing Activities

What kinds of projects can you undertake with desktop publishing? Here is a sample of actual projects from around the country:

• At Westlake High School in California, journalism students use desktop publishing to produce the school newspaper. Teachers report that the use of desktop publishing encourages students to be more creative and experiment more in the design process. Another benefit of desktop publishing is that it gives students increased control of their work. Instead of the teacher having to make many of the decisions, students are now responsible for the entire publication process.

• The Oklahoma City Public Schools produce a series of family learning guides in the form of calendars that are intended to strengthen the home/school partnership. The calendars contain daily activities that parents and children can do to reinforce what is being taught at school. More than 125,000 of these calendars are distributed in about 25 counties.

• Students of Christ the King School in South Bend, Indiana produced a book entitled *Special Places In and Around Michiana* which contained student descriptions and illustrations of hundreds of locations or events in the Michigan and Indiana area. Most of the descriptions were based on family trips.

• Many vocational educational programs have adopted desktop publishing as a major curriculum activity. For example, Bell High School in Bell, California has established an Electronic Publishing Instructional Center (EPIC) that provides students with "real world" experience producing posters, newsletters, and flyers for local businesses and organizations. Students in these programs have no problem finding jobs at newspapers or advertising agencies!

• Elementary teachers in hundreds of schools use simple desktop publishing programs to have their students create class newspapers that are woven into curriculum activities. For example, at the Wickliffe Elementary School in Columbus, Ohio, students in two classes studying the Wild West produced the *Western Weekly*. Second graders produced a series of brochures explaining pet care and training. Third and fourth graders studying Greece created a travel brochure.

• Production of school yearbooks or literary magazines using desktop publishing technology is becoming commonplace. At New Hartford Central High School in New York, students from word processing classes team up with the school's poetry club to publish *Inspirations*, a magazine of student poetry. At the Pullen Arts Magnet School in Landover, Maryland, desktop publishing is used to produce a student literary magazine, *Vignettes*, a quarterly school newspaper, and for an annual Write-a-Book contest.

Writing and Publishing a Magazine

Newark InDepth is a magazine written and published by the young men of St. Benedict's Preparatory School in Newark, New Jersey.(See Figure 4-3). It features investigative reports, personal interviews, graphics and photographs exploring the events that precipitated the violent summer of 1967. The faculty moderators include Jack Dougherty, Keith Corpus, and Father Malachy McFadden. In the course of creating the magazine, the students learned computer and desktop publishing skills. They developed interviewing and research skills while interviewing community members, police, store owners, and residents. The students also used the resources of the Newark Public Library.

The students wrote their articles after several iterations. The faculty chose the subject but the students quickly became enthusiastic because of the "lack of knowledge about that period among Newarkers."

Figure 4-3 Students write and publish a magazine

Students used black and white photos and political cartoons. The learned how to use computer graphics as they depicted the climate of the city in the spring and summer of 1967. They included articles describing police brutality, looting, and the destruction of the city. One student, Brian James, age 15, wrote, "the brutality occurred so often that it seemed like . . . a requirement for the police to beat up on minorities."

Another issue of *Newark InDepth* focused on toxic waste in Newark. This issue included an interview with Mayor Sharpe James on the subject of incinerators. A student, Omari Frazier, conducted the interview. He asked "What are the benefits of having it (the incinerator) in Newark besides benefiting financially?" The mayor replied: "Newark has more garbage than anyone else, and if we didn't have it in Newark we would have to pay to take it somewhere else. If it were not in Newark we wouldn't receive a host benefit fee. I also like to think that during the construction phase there were construction jobs for Newark residents and after it's built, there will be permanent jobs. Because it's an uninvited guest we tried to make the best of the situation."

Summary

Like the use of word processing for writing activities, desktop publishing is a computer use that cuts across the curriculum. Common applications include: class/school newspapers, yearbooks, literary magazines, flyers, posters, handouts, and school calendars. Desktop publishing is especially relevant to vocational education and journalism classes. In many cases, desktop publishing projects allow students to expand their learning activities beyond the school walls.

The two key elements to desktop publishing are page layout software and a laser printer. Other components that you may want to take advantage of are clip art collections and a scanner or digitizer. Keep in mind that desktop publishing generally builds on the use of word processing and graphics creation programs, so it makes sense to learn these programs first before tackling desktop publishing.

Further Information

There are many books about desktop publishing. Some focus on a particular page layout program (such as Pagemaker, Print Shop, or Ventura); others discuss general techniques. There are also magazines devoted to the subject such as *Desktop Publishing* and *Publish*. Most educational computing magazines (see Chapter 14) often run articles about desktop publishing applications in the classroom.

Here are some books that focus on basic concepts and design issues in desktop publishing:

Black, R. (1991). *Roger Black's Desktop Design Power*. New York: Bantam.

Burns, D., Venit, S., & Hansen, R. (1988). *The Electronic Publisher*. New York: Brady.

Harris, R. (1990). *Understanding Desktop Publishing*. San Francisco: Sybex.

Parker, R. (1990). *Looking Good in Print: A Guide to Basic Design for Desktop Publishing* (2nd edition). Chapel Hill, NC: Ventana Press.

Williams, Robin. (1990). *The Mac Is Not a Typewriter.* Berkeley, CA: Peachpit Press.

Activities

- Have your students prepare a catalog based on some book or topic they have studied (or a catalog of real items they or their parents wish to sell). Each student should draw a picture of an item and write a description of it. Assign someone to assemble the catalog and someone to create a cover page.

- Ask your class to create a class yearbook. Pair students up to interview each other. As the year progresses, have the students write about holidays and special events. Let each student create a design for the cover; have the class vote on the design to be used. If you have a scanner or digitizer, include photographs of each student.

- Create a "Nursery Rhyme Newspaper." Have students write news stories about a nursery rhyme (or fairy tale) they have read. You might want to provide them with a worksheet that helps them identify who, what, where, when, etc. You also may want to have students analyze real newspaper articles to understand the important elements. Set up a newspaper format with a banner, headlines, and columns and load the student stories into it.

- Open a class "print shop" making and selling banners, flyers, or posters to the rest of the school. Organize the class as a company with sales representatives, a production manager, financial manager, etc. Have the students create all the forms needed to run the company as well as advertising materials. Use the income received to buy desktop publishing supplies and software!

- Have the class create a Welcome Manual for new students. Let students brainstorm the information that should be in the manual (including maps and photographs). Discuss the multicultural aspects of this project and consider publishing aspects of the guide in multiple languages.

Chapter 5
Breaking Down Walls

"The isolation of the classroom" is a characteristic of schooling that worries many teachers. On the one hand, the relative isolation of the classroom gives teachers and students the freedom to pursue learning and teaching in a relatively uninterrupted way, without the intrusion of day-to-day events from the outside world. On the other hand, more and more teachers wish for a convenient means to connect with people, ideas, and information in the outside world. The teachers in this chapter are discovering that the combination of computers and telecommunications—called telecomputing—can provide that convenient window on the world they are looking for.

These teachers have many different reasons for telecomputing. Some want to collaborate with other teachers who share similar interests or problems, whether those colleagues are in the same building, school district, state, country, or elsewhere in the world. Some want to provide their students with real and diverse audiences for their activities. Some want to promote collaborative learning. Others find that they and their students need access to information or expertise that is not available in their school building or local community. With the increasing interdependency of people around the world, teachers everywhere are looking for ways to enable their students to have firsthand contact with students and adults from other cultures (see Chapter 8). Some teachers are providing their students access to remote equipment, such as remote sensors or supercomputers. With the increasing pace of change in science and technology, teachers are looking for new mechanisms for updating curriculum content.

Teachers have to overcome many technical, economic, organizational, and pedagogical obstacles to using telecomputing either for their own professional development or for student learning. Yet thousands have been so motivated by the power of this medium that they have found ways to do so.

Coming to Terms with Telecommunications

What Is Telecomputing?

Telecomputing is a term that combines the ideas of computing and telecommunications. Another phrase sometimes used is "computer-mediated communications." The term "telecomputing" is being used to distinguish computer access at a distance from the more general term "telecommunications," which is often used to describe satellite-delivered or instructional television (ITV). The term "distance learning" may imply use of either or both technologies.

What Is a Modem?

In order for computers to connect to a remote network via telephone lines, a device called a modem is needed. The modem converts the digital information from the computer into analog information that can be sent over the telephone. Modems differ in the speed at which they send and receive information; the most common speed in use today is 1200 bits/second (baud). However, in the future the speed is likely to increase to 2400, 4800 or 9600 baud. Eventually, we will use all-digital telephone systems called ISDN and modems will not be needed.

What Is a LAN?

A local area network (LAN) is a group of computers that are physically connected or "hard wired" together. The computers can all be in the same room, building, or campus. Although modems are not required for a LAN, each computer must have an appropriate LAN interface card. It is common to dedicate one computer (called the "server") to the role of managing the network. In the past the most common uses of LANs in schools have been to share resources such as a printer or hard disk or to manage instruction via an integrated learning system. However, a schoolwide LAN can also be used to facilitate creative collaborations and new social organizations by helping teachers and students across subjects create work groups, share data, and collaborate with one another.

What Is a Remote Bulletin Board System?

A remote bulletin board system (RBBS) is a software system on a computer that allows people to read and post electronic messages. To connect to the RBBS, you simply dial the phone number through your modem. Since most bulletin boards involve a local phone call and do not charge any usage fees, they are an inexpensive form of telecommunications. Many private individuals, private organizations, and school districts set up bulletin board systems for a wide variety of purposes. RBBS software is relatively inexpensive and is available for most popular personal computers.

Technology for Telecomputing

Telecomputing as a communications technology has several characteristics that help teachers and students break through the isolation of the classroom in ways that are not feasible through other means. Telecomputing helps break down barriers to access and interaction with people, information, and other resources such as remote sensors and supercomputers—barriers of physical distance, time, organization, and culture.

Most obviously, interaction via telecomputing is independent of *distance.* When you interact with a person, group, database, remote sensor, or computer through your computer and a telecommunications network, it is (practically) irrelevant whether the person or technology resource is physically located in another room, building, town, state, or country. Telecommunications networks are interconnected throughout the world, although the technology is more advanced in some regions than others. For example, here is a message on the Apple Global Education (AGE) network from a teacher in Iceland looking for collaboration with colleagues on the opposite side of the planet:

Item 0489273 23-Sept-90 12:53PDT
From: ICE0004 ICEU Melaskoli, Reykjavik,AGE
To: AGE$ Apple Global Education
cc: AGE.RD$ Apple Global Education R&D
Sub: LOGO teachers, a teaser

LOGO teachers!
It must be that a considerable number of LOGO teachers are by now members of AGE. We have therefore irresistible opportunity to exchange opinions on various aspects of our common subject.
I suggest that we start by introducing us, I have heard from one already, Bob Lawler, and am certain that there will be more to join us in a LOGO conversation that is unique!
On a LOGO conference in MIT several years ago I saw that Australians had moved more than 100 FORWARD. I am looking FORWARD to hear from someone over there and from many more in other countries.
We can teach each other innumerable things, that is for sure.
Yours,
Ragnheidur Benediktsson
LOGO teacher in ICELAND

Second, telecomputing is more flexible with regard to *time* than other means of communication. Through telecommunications your interaction with people or information on other computers can be either immediate (sometimes referred to as "real time") or delayed in various ways. On the voice telephone, both parties need to be speaking to each other at the same real time, even if it's 2 p.m. at one speaker's location and 2 a.m. at the other's. With telecomputing, participants in a conversation can interact at a time convenient to them. This is particularly important in a school setting, where both teachers' and students' time is tightly scheduled on both a daily and a yearly basis. On the one hand, a teacher cannot be taking phone calls in the middle of class; on the other hand, the answer to a question is needed while the topic is still being addressed by the class.

A third critical characteristic of telecomputing is its flexibility with regard to *organization.* Groups can form or dissolve at any time for purposes shared by the members. Participants in an online community may be from schools, universities, industries, or governments. For example, Dr. Marvin Bratt, a professor at Ohio State University, describes his learning experiences in working with middle school children via telecommunications:

Early in March, I had noticed an appeal on the Apple Global Education bulletin board on AppleLink from David Allan of Marigold School in Victoria, British Columbia, Canada for mentors of sixteen middle school students who were to work on independent study projects. I discussed this with our university students and they seemed eager to accept the challenge, especially when we saw the students' pictures. We developed biographies for each of us, scanned photographs, and sent the package to Marigold for their consideration. They accepted our offer and the phone lines heated up. Our project was to be focused on Earth Day. Dave asked me for a list of the students on our end who were willing to mentor. I had also enlisted the aid of our physicist, two mathematicians, and an artist. I wanted to be prepared for anything! He then paired us up with students and projects on his end. For example, I worked with middle school students Garrett Stephenson and Darren Pendergast and they had chosen the topic "Driftnet Fishing."

Now I must be honest at this point . . . I had a vague notion about this topic but I was to learn a good deal in the process myself! Darren and Garrett sent me a preliminary outline of their project. I responded by looking through our Academic Index (a computerized listing of journal articles) and sending bibliographic citations of recent articles to them. Looking through some of the articles, I learned all about the problem of driftnet fishing. Little did I know that boats use nylon nets forty miles long to fish for tuna. Little did I know that these nets ensnare dolphins and other fish which are often destroyed in the process of bringing in the tuna. Back and forth went rough drafts and criticisms, questions and answers, comments from team members on each end of this distance learning experiment.

As Earth Day came closer and closer, we got more and more information from the network moderator who was spearheading the collection of articles on Earth Day from schools around the world. He collected all the articles that the cub reporters from the schools sent in. Then on Earth Day (Friday, April 20, for us) he streamed all the articles back out to the schools (similar to the Associated Press) where students were waiting to construct newspapers. These electronic newspapers were then shared on the network by all the member schools.

At Ohio State U, we were particularly interested in the articles the students from Marigold sent. To our surprise, they had done the articles and had constructed complex graphic posters as well! What a project, what an experience for us at Ohio State.

On a telecomputing network, such characteristics as a person's age, race, social position, wealth, professional status, and the like are invisible unless the members have an explicit reason to make them salient. Imagine the look on the ten-year-old's face when he reported the following to his teacher concerning an online collaboration he was having: "A college student on the network is teaching me how to design a space station . . . (pause) . . . and he doesn't know I'm just a little boy!"

Another very powerful characteristic of telecomputing is that the information sent or received is inherently *manipulable* by virtue of being in electronic form and by virtue of the fact that the communication is mediated by computer. This means that the user can store, modify, analyze, reformat, combine, and in all other ways control the information. To use the simplest example, children typically compose their electronic mail messages on their word processors and then transmit them via the electronic network to local or remote readers. In turn, the receivers can store the messages for later printing, reading, revising, or responding. The receiver can easily file a particular message with other material related to a topic or project. For writing comments on another person's message, various conventions are adopted. In the simplest example, a student playing the role of a peer critic or editor of another's message might intersperse comments in UPPERCASE TO DISTINGUISH THEM FROM THE ORIGINATOR'S WRITING. In more flexible systems such as the Macintosh, several authors of a document sometimes use different fonts **or boldface** to distinguish the different authors' comments.

Technology Opens Doors to the World

Peter MacLeod, the high school geography teacher profiled in Chapter 2, says, "There is a world out there, outside the school. Technology opens the doors to the world." With communications, students are reaching out to others. Peter's class is twinned with a class in Bologna, Italy. The children are comparing the environmental concerns of their respective communities.

During the fall semester of 1989, Jeff Golub's debate class at Shorecrest High School in Seattle, Washington was enrolled in the AT&T Long Distance Learning Network. They were assigned to a learning circle made up of seven other participating classrooms. Five of their electronic partners were from other parts of the United States and two were from West Germany. "During the fall semester, the Berlin Wall came tumbling down, and we received eyewitness reports from our electronic partners in West Germany." A student at the Marie-Curie-Oberschule in Berlin wrote frequently, answering other students' questions and giving a valuable perspective of the historic events unfolding in his city. "Through such exchanges of information, we helped each other investigate various global issues and prepare reports that described our findings and insights."

The whole project was characterized by a sense that we had a real purpose and a real audience for our writing and research and communication. Each morning I posted in our classroom the latest notes from our electronic partners, and the students were thus reminded daily that there really were other students and classrooms out there who were eager to hear from us and had things to say themselves .... The LDLN program represents a cooperative community effort, a way of learning that will be characteristic of instruction in the schools for the twenty-first century. Through this telecommunications project, we were able to explore and experience the future of education.

Online Information Retrieval

Erica Lodish, a media specialist at Blair High School in Silver Spring, Maryland, has played a key role in her school helping other teachers and students learn how to access information and people outside the walls of the school. Erica works with teachers and students in three phases. First, she works with ninth graders and their teachers to build basic skills in online searching. Second, she works with selected classroom teachers to create whole-class projects in specific subject areas. Third, she works with individual students engaged in independent projects.

With the ninth grade novices, Erica and the classroom teachers introduce the basic concepts and skills involved in defining a research question, identifying the kinds of information needed, planning a search strategy, and going online to search for the information. She has developed special worksheets to structure these activities. In collaborating with classroom teachers on curriculum-based projects, Erica has found it productive to work closely with each teacher to clarify their respective roles and responsibilities. They developed a teacher collaboration worksheet form to plan the project and their respective teaching responsibilities in it.

The high school students' independent work on their science fair projects and senior projects provides compelling examples of the value of online information retrieval. The students first perform background research in their area of interest, using online databases. Topics have included:

- Biochemistry: electrical stimulus to speed regeneration of tissue.
- Computer science: develop hardware to recognize voice.
- Physics: application of magnetism to transportation devices.
- Neurobiology: neurotransmitters.
- Microbiology: laser fluorescence to study tissue response.

Students are able to locate current literature in these rapidly changing interdisciplinary subject areas by applying the skills Erica has helped them to acquire in searching online databases on DIALOG and CD-ROM encyclopedias and databases. The program provides the students with instant retrieval of current bibliographic information updated daily in hundreds of large databases used by professional scientists, engineers and businesspeople, such as Congressional Record Abstracts, Consumer Drug Information, Current Technology Index, MEDLINE, UPI News, and so on. They use the abstracts and descriptors from the bibliographic printouts to identify key concepts and terms for further background searching and to identify documents they need to read for their research.

The library/media center has made arrangements with several professional libraries in its geographic region to allow students to obtain specialized periodicals and books not available in the school or public libraries. Some students also use the online databases to locate scientists and engineers in their region who are specializing in the same area of research that the student wishes to work in. In many cases local telephone calls to the scientists from the students or their teachers have resulted in successful mentor relationships for these students.

Peter MacLeod's geography classes use a graphics-interface statistical database called Telichart for data from Statistics Canada's database. He encourages "lateral thinking" with the aid of the databases. In geography he starts the class with the online database running. He introduces a topic, such as the pulp and paper industry in Canada. The students find data they think are relevant in the database and produce a variety of graphs and charts. They print the charts. They brainstorm the topic, bringing into the discussion their prior knowledge. Taking off from the data the kids get and the ideas they contribute to the discussion, he then summarizes what the class has learned for the day.

Peter says, "Students love to use very large databases. If they can't find exactly what they are looking for, they really enjoy searching using a variety of alternative paths. There are always surprises. They also love to redesign the graphs until their ideas are shown as clearly as possible. Both the well-designed graphic interface and the use of color allow them to locate, display, and interpret data they consider meaningful."

Breaking Down Classroom Walls

Paul Reese has taught for twenty-one years at the Ralph Bunche Elementary School in central Harlem, New York. A major reason for his unusual persistence in this career is the mission he has been undertaking for the past eight years—creating a local area network (LAN) that is the catalyst for creativity among teachers and all 650 students throughout the grades 3-6 school. He designed the LAN to make possible the "serious integration of computer-based tools by kids and teachers" and highly creative collaborations among teachers in the school.

Most LANs in schools are designed for individual student work, and the LAN structure focuses on particular software or "courseware." Paul's network is designed to support collaboration. Thus, when students log on to the network (called "Earth Lab"), they are presented with a choice of access to their own private folders or folders shared with other students.

"What is important," Paul says, "is that they are not launching programs; they're making decisions about data. Kids should be encouraged to work together on computers and to create and share databases." The system recognizes three kinds of groups: the group that shares access to a common workspace, the group that receives mail under a common alias, and the group of individuals currently logged in at the computer. The first two kinds of groups are familiar in many office environments. The availability of the group workspaces actually helps promote collaborative work across the school. Teachers, for example, find it easier to assign projects to groups because of the existence of the shared workspace. The electronic aliases for the groups turned into a way to send out puzzles or "think-tank questions" for the group to work on. Having a shared workspace makes it convenient to construct large databases through the contributions of the many groups.

Paul Reese was named *Electronic Learning*'s 1990 "Teacher of the Year" for his creative and pioneering work with LANs.

Overcoming Obstacles

Thousands of teachers are involved in telecomputing, and most of them had to overcome quite a few obstacles in order to begin. For some of them, just getting access to a computer, a modem, and telecommunications software was a project in itself. For others, the equipment was readily available but getting access to a telephone in school was a long complicated process. Indeed, some teachers do the communications from their home computers instead of trying to get access to a phone at school. In addition to equipment, software, and phone lines, teachers often have to locate some technical assistance. Fortunately, some schools and school districts have library media specialists or computer coordinators who provide such assistance.

If the phone call is a local one and the online resource or community being used does not charge a fee, then the main cost of telecomputing is the teacher's time. This is why many teachers begin their first telecomputing activities by calling remote bulletin boards in their local calling area. However, if the teacher wants to use a commercial service—such as DIALOG for large databases or the National Geographic Kids Network—then there is the inevitable lobbying for funds from the school or district, or the search for outside sponsors of the activity. Some teachers have found creative ways of getting funding, such as getting a local business to sponsor a school's participation in Kids Network (see discussion of this network in Chapter 6).

After getting the necessary hardware, software, communications lines, and technical know-how, the next obstacle involves learning to use the particular online service or network resources. In a few cases, such as Kids Network, the user interface is especially designed for educational purposes and requires very little time to learn to use. At the other extreme are networks and bulletin boards whose user interfaces are so obscure that one must have extremely high motivation and persistence to learn to use them.

Technical and economic barriers are not the only obstacles to effective and successful educational use of telecomputing. As with any innovation, there are often false starts and experiments that don't work the first time. Margaret Riel and Jim Levin describe an early (around 1980) frustrating attempt in creating a "computer pals" network:

> *Our first thoughts on how to use computer networking to improve students' writing was to get them to write letters to one another. We realized that students in different cultural and geographic regions could provide one another with valuable contrasts to their taken-for-granted assumptions about the world. With the help of Ron Scollon in Alaska, we sought computer pals for students in California. Teachers collected "computer pal" messages from their students and these letters were sent by computer to classrooms in distant places.*
>
> *Students in Alaska and California were very excited about sending letters to their computer pals but matching large numbers of students in one-to-one relationships was problematic. The schools in Alaska had many fewer students so that letters from a single California classroom were distributed to four or five different schools. This resulted in time differences for responses with some students never receiving responses. Letters that came addressed with the general greeting "Dear Computer Pal" were not eagerly received by students who were awaiting personal responses. After six months of frustrations with the organization of the group and teacher dissatisfaction with the limited nature of the task, we abandoned the idea of computer pals.*

Their experience with the failed computer pals project led Riel, Levin, and others to create different kinds of online communities and tasks for learners. They set up a children's newswire network to encourage students to write and edit stories for publication in school newspapers. The task had an expected end product and there was a deadline for completion of stories. A network coordinator organized the sending and receiving of the students' work. She also sent press cards and blackline masters for the layout and production of the local versions of the students' newspapers.

The support and organization provided by the network coordinator seemed to be an important factor in keeping the network functioning. Students were excited to think of their stories being read by students across the country and around the world. They were especially excited when a story they wrote appeared in a newspaper from another school. The newswire continued for years as a successful example of computer networking in schools, and many electronic educational communities now use this format. The one-to-many or many-to-many group structure was easier to manage on a network and resulted in more communication and learning opportunities for the students.

Many teachers have come up with creative, important ideas for learning activities and posted these ideas on electronic networks, only to be disappointed in the outcome. Projects can fail for a variety of reasons, causing disappointment and frustration not only for the teacher but also for the students. Fortunately, the factors contributing to successful educational telecomputing activities are becoming more well understood as more teachers and researchers gain experience. The references listed at the end of this chapter provide valuable information to build on.

The FrEdMail Network

FrEdMail (Free Educational Electronic Mail) is a distributed network created by Al Rogers. Its primary purpose is to transmit student writing in batches from one place to another. In the middle of the night all the nodes in the network automatically dial each other and exchange messages. Students generally do their writing offline in the context of class projects or assignments and do not correspond with one another directly as in other networks. Here is a sample of a FrEdMail session:

```
Dialing...
ATDT19195978528
CONNECT 1200

CMS 12.61
===========================================================
=== W E L C O M E   T O ===================================
===========================================================
 _____        _____       _   __   __          _   _
!  ___!      !  ___!     ! ! ! \_/   !        !_! ! !
! !__   _    ! !___   ___! ! ! !\_/! !         _  ! !
!  __! ! !_  ! ___!  !  _  ! ! !   ! !  /\    ! ! ! !  _
! !    !  _! ! !___  ! !_! ! ! !   ! ! /   \  ! ! ! !_! !
!_!    !_!   !_____! !_____! !_!   !_!/_/\_\  !_! !_____!
```

```
===========================================================
            PERSON COUNTY SCHOOLS' LINK TO THE
     FREDMAIL EDUCATIONAL TELECOMMUNICATIONS NETWORK
                    300/1200/2400 BAUD
          RUSSELL DIXON & BARBARA LONG, SYSOP'S
===========================================================

TYPE 'NEW' TO SET UP A USER ACCOUNT.
TYPE 'GUEST' TO BROWSE AROUND.
OR TYPE YOUR USERNAME TO LOGIN.

USERNAME: NEW
CAN YOU RECEIVE LOWER CASE? Y


           ***************************************
           *             WELCOME TO              *
           *        PERSON COUNTY SCHOOLS'       *
           *        COMPUTER MAIL SERVICE        *
           *                                     *
           *              FrEdMail               *
 _________________________________________________
|                                                 |
| This Electronic Bulletin Board serves the needs |
| of educators, students, and the computing       |
| public in this community.                       |
|   ______________________________________________|_
|_|                                                 |
  | Access to this board is restricted to teachers, |
  | students, and responsible citizens of this      |
  | community who have bonafide interests in        |
  | education.                                      |
  |     ____________________________________________|___
  |__|                                                  |
     | You are welcome to log on and browse around.     |
     | However, if you want to receive a Validated      |
     | Account which grants full access to all of the   |
     | features of this board you must answer a few     |
     | questions about yourself.                        |
     |__________________________________________________|


Type your first name: BEVERLY
Enter your last name: HUNTER

Logging Caller #4845 On Jul 5, 1990, 11:54 AM...
On Line: BHUNTER : HUNTER, BEVERLY
0 Calls; Last Call: Jan 0, 1900, 12:00 AM
          Mail ABCDEFGHIJK
```

```
Access Lvl: 8  55505055000

*** NEWS BULLETIN ***
Headline: T H E   9 0 '   R E M E M B E R S
Date: Jan 20, 1990, 11:17 AM

 _______________________________________________
|                                               |
|              REMEMBER THE 90'S                |
|                                               |
| No we haven't just stepped out of a time      |
| machine or a bad dream.| We're asking         |
| students to use their imaginations and write  |
| the news stories they would most like to see  |
| in the coming decade.                         |
|                                               |
| The best stories will be telecommunicated to  |
| the central office for publishing/printing.   |
| The COURIER TIMES has also agreed to          |
| cooperate toward the possible publishing of   |
| the very best stories.                        |
|                                               |
| A formal proposal for this project has been   |
| posted in the NCIDEAS bulletin board.         |
|                                               |
| If you are interested in participating in     |
| this motivating project, call Barbara Long or |
| David Warlick at the central office           |
| (599-2191).                                   |
|_______________________________________________|

Time Now: Jul 5, 1990, 11:55 AM
30 Minutes Left
[Main Cmd: ABCEFGHKMNOPSTU?] ?
A <A>djust terminal settings
B <B>ulletin Boards
C <C>all Sysop for <C>hat
E <E>Mail
F <F>eature Articles
G <G>oodbye (Log Off)
H <H>elp
K <K>nowledgeable user (toggle)
M <M>ap of FrEdMail Network
N <N>ews Bulletins
O <O>pinion poll (once only)
P Change <P>assword
S <S>can New Msgs on Bulletin Boards
T <T>ime
U <U>ser Database
?
```

```
[Main Cmd: ABCEFGHKMNOPSTU?] E
Load EMAIL...2116K left in EMAIL
You have 0 Msgs
29 Minutes Left
3335
[EMAIL: BHKRSTUQ?]T
Send Msg.6729
To:   DWARLICK@PERSON%NCAROLINA
Subj: teacher contact
[Attach a file?: YN]N

Type msg (100 lines, 80 Chrs)
Type 3 RETURNS when done
  1: I read your article about the shopping project in the FRedMail
  2:News.  This is my first time on FRedMail, though I have talked
  3:to Al Rogers about it many times.
  4:I am writing a book about teachers and the ways in which they
  5:use computers in their work and teaching.  I would like to talk
  6:to a teacher who has been involved in the shopping project
  7:you described.  Can you give me a phone number for a teacher
  8:you could suggest, whose experiences would be interesting and
  9:informative for other teachers to read about? Thanks a lot!
 10:

[Edit: ACDEFHIKLSU?]?
 <A>dd Lines to Msg
 <C>ancel (Abort) Msg
 <D>elete Line
 <E>dit Line
 <F>ind Word or Phrase
 Edit <H>eader (To & Subj lines)
 <I>nsert Line
 <K>nowledgeable User
 <L>ist Msg
 <S>end or <S>ave Msg
 <U>pload Attached File

[Edit: ACDEFHIKLSU?]S
Msg.6729..Saved!
2115K left in EMAIL
You have 0 Msgs
23 Minutes Left
3218
[EMAIL: BHKRSTUQ?]B

Which Board (? for List): ?
A - IDEAS: Idea Exchange
B - KIDWIRE: Kid Wire
C - NEWS: System News
```

```
D - Private
E - NCIDEAS: N. C. Ideas
F - Private
G - SPEAK: SPEAK Project
H - SCI: Science
I - Private
J - Private
K - Private

Which Board (? for List): A
Load IDEAS...2115K left in IDEAS
[IDEAS: 37 Msgs: 1278 to 1314]
You have 37 new Msgs
22 Minutes Left
3423
[IDEAS: BEHKRSTQ?]S

Last Msg Read: 1
RETURN Scans From Msg.1, or Type New Msg # To Begin Search:
1290  :IDEAS   LSNEPP:OAKSCHL BOARD            06/08/90 [346]
1291  :IDEAS   MDIETZ:summer computer camp    06/08/90 [576]
1292  :IDEAS   JKRANS:Your Project             06/12/90 [241] (1 Files)
1293  :IDEAS   JKRANS:Projects                 06/12/90 [334] (1 Files)
1294  :IDEAS   DSAPP:summer school             06/12/90 [334]
1295  :IDEAS   AROGERS:NECC FrEdMail Gathering 06/13/90 [725]
1296  :IDEAS   TDOLAN:Computers in Australia?  06/14/90 [930]
1297  :IDEAS   JLEVIN:Livable Places Project   06/14/90 [1727]
1298  :IDEAS   DMEAD:HYPERSTUDIO STACK EXCHANG 06/15/90 [207]
1299  :IDEAS   DSPATOLA:Diablo S11 printer     06/15/90 [286]
1300  :IDEAS   FTOPPING:Polish Pianist Master! 06/15/90 [1676]
1301  :IDEAS   MUCHIDA:Alaskan Shopping Survey 06/16/90 [168]
1302  :IDEAS   DHARKINS:Irish Heritage       06/18/90 [563] (1 Files)
[IDEAS: 37 Msgs: 1278 to 1314]
You have 37 new Msgs
21 Minutes Left
3344
[IDEAS: BEHKRSTQ?]R 1295

Last Msg Read: 1
RETURN Scans From Msg.1, or Type New Msg # To Begin Search: 1295
1295 :IDEAS   AROGERS:NECC FrEdMail Gathering06/13/90 [725][RSDQ?]
Msg.1295
To:   &IDEAS@PERSON
From: &IDEAS@BLADEN
Path: BLADEN!SDCOE!AROGERS
Sent: 06/12/90  8:24 PM
Rcvd: 06/13/90  1:29 AM
Subj: NECC FrEdMail Gathering
```

```
Copies: $SYSOPS,$IDEAS

It's getting mighty close now!

I hope you're planning on attending NECC 90 in Nashville!
If so, DON'T forget the FrEdMail Birds of a Feather session
scheduled for Monday evening.
Time and place will be found on the "Birds of a Feather"
bulletin board where you register.    Look for it, and BE THERE!
One of the things I'll do is to show you the new
TELESENSATIONS book and the brand new training module, T'nT
(Telecomputing and Teachers).... with 3 video tapes and software!
Hot stuff.  Great way to meet other FrEdMail users, too!

See you there.
Al Rogers
FrEdMail Central

Time Now: Jul 5, 1990, 12:15 PM
10 Minutes Left
[Main Cmd: ABCEFGHKMNOPSTU?]G


   _________________________
  !         LEAVING          !
  !    The Person County     !
  !         Schools          !_____
  !      FrEdMail Link       !    /
  !                          !   /
  !__________________________!  /
        /____!!_______________/
             !!   //
             !!  //
             !! //
             !!//
We Hope That You Enjoyed Yourself
     and will be back soon!
        DAVID WARLICK
  AND RUSSELL DIXON, SYSOPS

Logged on:  Jul 5, 1990, 11:54 AM

Logged off: Jul 5, 1990, 12:24 PM
Thank You for Calling, BHUNTER

Hanging Up...
NO CARRIER

+++ATH
```

Summary

Telecomputing breaks down walls. These could be walls between schools in different countries or walls between classrooms in the same school. As the stories in this chapter illustrate, teachers are using computer networks in many ways to let their students have greater access to others. Online information retrieval provides access to hundreds of databases and new resources. However, telecomputing often involves many obstacles to overcome. It's a new way of teaching and learning—one that will take time for our school system to get used to.

Further Information

Listed below are some books that will provide you with further background on telecommunications and networks. Chapter 12 provides the addresses of the networks mentioned in this chapter.

Andres, Y., Jacks, M., & Rogers, A. (1989). *Telesensations: The Educators' Handbook to Instructional Telecomputing*. Bonita, CA: FrEdMail Foundation.

Bowen, C., & Peyton, D. (1990) *The Complete Electronic Bulletin Board Starter Kit*. New York: Bantam. [Includes BBS software for IBM PCs.]

Clark, Chris, Kurshan, Barbara, & Yoder, Sharon. (1989). *Telecommunications in the Classroom.* Eugene, OR: International Society for Technology in Education.

Dvorak, J. (1990). *Dvorak's Guide to PC Telecommunications.* New York: McGraw-Hill. [Includes disks for PC.]

Glossbrenner, A. (1990). *The Handbook of Personal Computer Communications (3rd edition).* New York: St. Martin's Press.

Harasim, Linda.(1989). *Online Education.* New York: Praeger.

Hunter, Beverly, & Lodish, Erica. (1989) *Online Searching in the Curriculum.* Santa Barbara, CA: ABC-Clio, Inc.

Mason, R,. & Kaye., A. (1989). *Mindweave: Communications, Computers and Distance Education.* New York: Pergamon Press.

Office of Technology Assessment. (1989). *Linking for Learning*. Washington, DC: Government Printing Office, Document 052-003-01170-1.

Quarterman, John S. (1990). *The Matrix: Computer Networks and Conferencing Systems Worldwide*. Bedford, MA: Digital Press.

Roberts, Nancy, Blakeslee, George, Brown, Maureen, & Lenk, Cecelia. (1990). *Integrating Telecommunications into Education*. Englewood Cliffs, NJ: Prentice-Hall.

Activities

• Sign on to an educator's electronic forum or conference on a large network or bulletin board system. Make a substantive contribution to at least one discussion on the forum.

• Download a portion of a discussion from an online educator's forum or conference. Offline, call up these files on a word processor in a class setting to "simulate" being online, to expose other members of your class to an example of that network activity.

• Use an online database such as ERIC to locate reports about educational uses of telecommunications.

• Gather information concerning three different educational telecomputing services. Compare the pros and cons of these for use in your class/school situation. Take into account the following criteria in addition to others you wish to add: costs, initial and continuing; fixed or variable; purposes for which used, in relation to your purposes; subject areas addressed; technical skill levels required to use, in relation to technical skill levels of the users in your situation; who is available to collaborate with on this service, in relation to your purposes.

• Find out what the phrase "virtual classroom" means. What research has been conducted to advance our understanding of factors contributing to the effectiveness of virtual classrooms?

Chapter 6
Scientists at Work

Science is a process, a way of looking at the world and seeking understanding of it. Basically, it is a process of observing some aspect of the world, asking questions about that aspect, proposing answers, testing answers against available evidence, trying to make sense of the data, and continuing to ask more refined questions. The best way for students to learn science is to *do* science—to participate, engage in, the processes we call "science."

At the same time, learners must understand fundamental concepts if they are to be able to make sense of the data they gather and analyze. It is not easy for learners to give up their own intuitive, naive conceptions about how the world works in favor of the conceptions that modern scientists agree on. The teachers described in this chapter are employing computer-based systems in diverse ways to help address these twin goals of moving the processes of classroom science closer to those of real science, and of moving the learners toward conceptions of the natural world that more closely match the explanations that scientists hold.

Technology for Science Education

To support science education, technology must support the doing of science. This includes:

• Instruments such as temperature probes and motion detectors for taking measurements of physical phenomena.
• Tools such as databases, spreadsheets, and graphing programs for recording, storing, interpreting, and analyzing data.
• Techniques such as modeling, simulations, video and image processors for visualizing phenomena not visible to the naked eye because of speed, distance, size, complexity, or inaccessibility.
• Programs such as word processors, databases, HyperCard, and electronic networks for communicating and collaborating with colleagues.

NGS Kids Network: Doing Real Science

Tens of thousands of elementary and middle school children and their teachers are contributing to the scientific body of knowledge about acid rain, among other socially significant scientific matters, as they participate in a project called Kids Network sponsored by the National Geographic Society. This project has clearly demonstrated to students, teachers, administrators, parents, and science educators that students and their teachers can engage in meaningful scientific investigations while they learn both the concepts and processes of science.

In Kids Network, the students (grades 4-6) and their teacher in one classroom collaborate with students and teachers in other classrooms around the country and the world as they investigate issues of interest to them and their communities. The Acid Rain project is the most well developed of these investigations, having been refined by thousands of teachers, students, and researchers since 1986. The children are introduced to the concept of pH through hands-on experiments in which they measure the ph of common substances such as vinegar, cola drinks, and tap water. Small teams of students build an apparatus to collect rainwater in their own backyards or school yard. They also collect water in local streams and lakes.

The teams measure the pH of their samples and enter their values into a database on the computer. They compare the values they have found among the teams in a class and discuss differences in data across teams and samples. Next they transmit their database to a scientist on the Kids Network, who comments on their data in relation to the data gathered by children in other classes. The students then download the data from other classes, which they compare using a variety of tools for analysis.

Bruce MacDonald, one of the early Kids Network teachers, is enthusiastic about this approach because his students are involved in a socially important topic to which they can make a real scientific contribution. Like many other elementary teachers he had a liberal arts major in college and had a minimal science background. He feels that by having his students work on meaningful projects with the support of good teaching materials, he has no difficulty comprehending the science involved. He also enjoys being able to have projects in which he and his students can connect science to mathematics and social studies. The fact that students all across the country are participating in the project makes the idea of science as a collective enterprise become a reality to him and his students.

Sue Mundi, another Kids Network teacher from Flemington, New Jersey, points out that such projects are not only interesting to students, but to teachers as well. Much of her enthusiasm for Kids Network comes from the fact that this project-oriented work connects to her personal interests. "I'm pleased to be part of Kids Network because this activity is an educational adventure which incorporates my personal concern (the environment), my personal goal (becoming more familiar with computers), my personal belief that the youth of today must learn of problems now in order to be successful adult leaders, and my professional philosophy that subjects should not be taught in isolation."

Innovation Involves Trial and Error

Jeanne Meadows teaches earth science at Langley High School in Fairfax County, Virginia. She says, "Kids need to understand that innovation involves trial and error. If that isn't science, what is?" Every year for the past several years Jeanne and her students have tried out one or more kinds of computer-based activities in science class. Her students sometimes find themselves in the position of "debuggers" of innovative activities and technology. For example, last year she got her ninth graders involved in two experimental projects. One, a telecomputing "Star Schools" project, involved sharing weather information via telecommunications with students in schools throughout the world. There were many technical difficulties with the telecommunications network, including getting disconnected at unexpected times, no automatic redial for the network, and being assigned to a low priority by the network

Photo : Michael Lessin

so they would get "bumped off" the line. They were shipped the wrong module of print materials. When they finally did connect with the working group, they had a backlog of far too many messages for them to read and analyze in the school time available to them. At the same time, their school was being renovated, they had to move their equipment and classes several times, and they lost their access to the telephone. Nevertheless, Jeanne expects to participate again next year. "We'll give it one more try," she says.

Gathering, Sharing, and Analyzing Data

Jeanne is also working with her students in a project initiated by the science coordinator in their county to monitor water quality in the Potomac River. Her class is collaborating with students from seven other county schools. Each class takes water samples from a different location of the river, including sites above, in, and below the city of Washington D.C. They measure such water characteristics as temperature and amount of dissolved oxygen, carbon dioxide, phosphates, nitrates, and coliform bacteria and temperature. They take these measurements four times a year and enter their data into a special forum on their county's Remote Bulletin Board System. The students then perform comparative analyses on the collective database.

Jeanne believes that in their lifetimes these students will not be able to ignore issues such as water quality, and that the skills and knowledge they are developing now will be important to them throughout their lives, whatever their occupations. She believes it is important for students to be able to manipulate data and make sense of it as they formulate their own questions and attempt to find answers. This was the central reason why she volunteered in the 1988-89 school year to field test with her previous seventh grade classes a Hypercard-based program called Scientists at Work. In this program the students play the roles of research assistants at a nature center. They work in groups to formulate their own research questions and attempt to synthesize answers to the questions by using a database of animals and the tools for manipulating data contained in the program.

Visualizing Biology With Animation, Videodisc, and Video-microscopes

Russ Doren, a science teacher at Cherry Creek High School in Aurora, Colorado uses a range of media and tools to help his students visualize processes in biology. He developed a set of HyperCard stacks to use as extra credit assignments. The five stacks cover cancer, cell mitosis and meiosis, bacteria, and cell parts. Two of his stacks include animation from a VideoWorks file he wrote on animating the process of cell division. What was originally intended to be simply a demo program on cell division ended up being incorporated interactively into two of his HyperCard stacks. The students check out the software in the library and run the programs on the library's Macintosh computers. After seeing how easy it is to use HyperCard, most students complete computer assignments and agree that "computers aren't something that they have to be scared of." Many students end up completing assignments on all five of the programs. Now he encourages students to write simple HyperCard stacks as extra credit for biology assignments.

In order to help his department keep up with changes in video technology, Russ spearheaded efforts to purchase and install a set of 27" high-resolution color monitors in three classrooms. Not only has the equipment been used for videotapes, it has also been used for an interactive computer videodisc system and two videomicroscopy setups he helped establish. Whenever he runs a lab involving microscopes, he hooks a videomicroscope unit to a demo microscope and projects the image on the color monitors. "Now the students know exactly what to look for, whether we are viewing cell parts, plant anatomy, or pond organisms."

Russ received a $2,000 district grant for instituting an interactive videodisc system in his department. The system included a hard drive for the Macintosh computer, a Pioneer LDV-4200 videodisc player, and a BioSci videodisc with HyperCard stackware. The BioSci videodisc contains over 5,000 color slides covering at least 17 different areas of biological science and can be used all year.

Russ has compiled slide shows on animal taxonomy and runs his slide shows on specific animal groups while lecturing on details of each group. He has also had great success using the videodisc for a discussion of cell division through the use of the disc's short film sequence on mitosis. Using a graphic remote control on the Mac's screen, he runs the video backward and forward, as well as being able to stop the action in order for the students to understand the process of mitosis thoroughly. For the second half of class, he conducts a lab on cell mitosis using onion root tips. He demonstrates how to prepare a slide and projects a slide on the video monitors using a videomicroscope unit. The students then prepare their own slides and successfully complete the lab.

Russ feels that interactive videodisc technology is here to stay. His advanced placement biology classes also use the interactive setup. He has put two more laserdiscs and stackware an upgrade to the BioSci videodisc into his next year's budget. His library has also put together an interactive video system and plans to check it out to other departments in the school.

The Computer as Lab Partner

"Science is all about solving problems," says Doug Kirkpatrick, Science teacher at Foothill Intermediate School, Walnut Creek, California. He uses microcomputer-based laboratory (MBL) tools to provide his students the opportunity to become real experimenters. In contrast to traditional science labs where the experiment has been designed by the teacher or the lab book writer, in Doug's classes the students design their own experiments. Doug provides the students with a problem situation that is interesting to them, and it is up to them to set up experiments to address the problem. For example, the students had to plan and conduct a series of experiments to determine the variables that would affect the design of a swimming pool such that a minimum amount of money would be required to keep the pool warm. Similarly, students work on problems such as determining what material would best keep a baked potato warm or how to house an alien being whose body temperature must be kept at 10 degrees.

Doug likes the students to use MBL because they can focus on the physical environment they are experimenting with "while the computer does the mundane drudgery kinds of calculations." He is continually surprised at how much time students spend on task when working on problems of interest to them. At the same time, he observes them improving their communication skills and developing an understanding of critical concepts such as the difference between heat and temperature.

What Is an MBL?

Microcomputer-based laboratory (MBL) tools were first developed at the Technical Education Research Center (TERC) in Cambridge, Massachusetts, under the direction of Bob Tinker. They make use of inexpensive probes connected to an Apple Macintosh or IBM PC computer through an interface box, to measure such physical quantities as temperature, position, velocity, acceleration, sound, current and voltage, light intensity, and ionizing radiation. Data are displayed in digital and graphical form on the computer monitor as the measurements are taken. Students can transform and analyze the data, print graphs or tables, or save data to disks for later analysis. The tools do not simulate physical phenomena but rather provide ways of representing reality. Students do not need to know anything about computers to use MBL tools. Students are in control of their learning since they select the measurements to be made and the way the data are displayed.

Motion detectors measure, display, and record the position, velocity, and acceleration of an object. The motion probe is essentially a sonar unit that transmits short pulses of high-frequency sound, then amplifies and detects the echo much as a bat is able to do. The computer is programmed to measure the time between the transmitted and received pulses and to calculate the position, velocity, and acceleration of the object. In a typical beginning experiment, students will watch their own motion being plotted as position, velocity, or acceleration graphs as they move away from and toward the motion detector.

The following characteristics of these tools have been found to be important to student learning (Thornton & Solokoff, 1991):

• The tools allow student-directed exploration but free students from most of the time-consuming drudgery associated with data collection and display.

• The data are plotted in graphical form in real time, so that students get immediate feedback and see the data in an understandable form.

• Because data are quickly taken and displayed, students can easily examine the consequences of a large number of changes in experimental conditions during a single laboratory period. The students spend a large portion of their laboratory time observing physical phenomena and interpreting, discussing and analyzing data.

• The hardware and software tools are general, independent of the experiments. The variety of probes use the same interface box and the same software format. Students are able to focus on the investigation of many different physical phenomena without spending large amounts of time learning to use complicated tools.

• The tools dictate neither the phenomena to be investigated, the steps of the investigation, nor the level or sophistication of the curriculum. Thus a wide range of students from elementary school to university level are able to use the same set of tools to investigate the physical world.

• Because data are presented in an understandable way, collaboration among students is encouraged.

MBL software and interfaces are available for most personal computers. For example, IBM markets the Personal Science Laboratory for IBM PCs and PS/2s that allows data collection for light, pH level, temperature and motion. Playing with Science from Sunburst Communications provides MBL capabilities for the Apple II. An extensive set of MBL programs for the Macintosh have been developed by the Workshop Physics Project at Dickinson College and the Scientific Thinking Projects at Tufts University. A Macintosh ULI (Universal Lab Interface) package and the programs developed in these projects are available from Vernier Software.

Laboratory-Based Physics

Malcolm Wells has been refining his approach to teaching high school physics over a period of many years. His physics courses are laboratory based. For a given phenomenon or concept in physics, his students first discuss the variables of interest (e.g., force and distance in a spring). They discuss what the dependent and independent variables would be in an experiment designed to help them create a mathematical model of the phenomenon. He shows them what equipment is available for the experiment, and they work in small groups to design and plan their experiments.

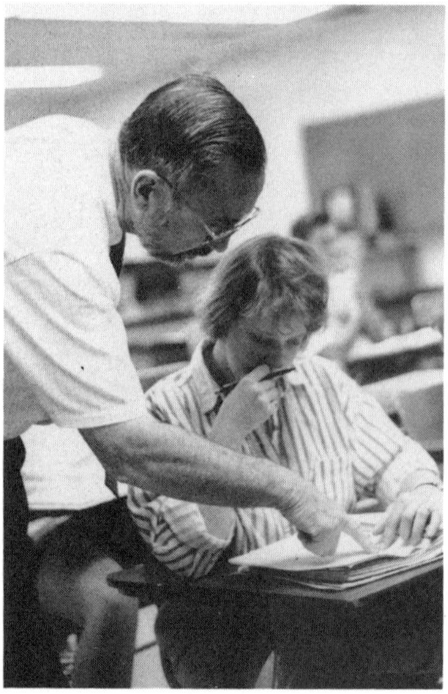

Each small group performs the experiment they have planned, using (usually) MBL equipment to capture and graph data such as distance, time, velocity, and so on. They interpret the graphs, then create a mathematical description of the graphs. They create an explanation of their experiment on their group's "white board" and then present their findings to the whole class.

Malcolm rarely lectures to the whole class. Most of the class time is spent with small groups either working on experiments or solving exercises. Also, he only assigns readings in the textbook *after* the students have had a chance to experiment with the phenomena. So the textbook reading becomes a kind of "wrap up" activity, a summary.

Over the years, Malcolm tried a variety of different computer applications to support his teaching. In the 1970s he started writing drill and practice programs and tried them on his students, but the programs didn't seem to be making enough difference. Then he tried writing some simulations of experiments his students couldn't do very well in the physics lab—e.g., on Coulomb's law. He still uses some of these, but again he did not see that they made much difference. Then about 1983 he started making his own interfaces to the Apple II+ for lab experiments—light sensors, and the like. This has proved to be highly productive, and now he cannot imagine how to teach physics without computers! Malcolm feels very strongly about the importance of the Apple II line of computers for his purposes. They suit his needs very well because of the open architecture, ease of building and connecting MBL interfaces, and ease of programming the interfaces.

Malcolm Wells is collaborating with David Hestenes, a physicist at the University of Arizona, on a National Science Foundation-supported project to teach his methods of teaching to other teachers in Arizona.

Keeping Current

Gloria Seelman, biology teacher at Montgomery Blair High School in Silver Spring, Maryland, was able to develop, in six summer weeks, thirteen large "topic notebooks" for a course she designed called "Current Topics in Biomedical Research." She was able to develop (and continues to update) this material so quickly because she had access to online databases through DIALOG. Examples of her topics include:

• Molecular biology: How is molecular biology providing evidence for evolution?

• Psychobiology: What is the relationship between cocaine, depression and brain chemistry?

• Membrane technology: What is the relationship between endosomes, proteins, and gap junctions in individualization of cellular activity?

• Gene activation and expression: What factors influence gene activation and expression?

• Circulatory system and technological advancement: What is the relationship between current medical technological research developments and the circulatory system?

Gloria is able to provide her students with current periodical literature on these rapidly changing topics from diverse scientific and social journals. She challenges the students to address the scientific, technological, social and ethical aspects of these issues. For example, one group of students used the online databases to locate a member of the Ethical Board of the National Institutes of Health and invited her to speak to the class about ethical issues involved in some of the recent biomedical developments. According to Gloria, it simply would not be feasible to provide such a course without the availability of the online search capability and the support of the Library Media program.

Real Science Requires Collaboration

In the summer of 1987 high school earth science teacher Bill Krayer worked as an intern at the Terrestrial Physics Laboratory at Goddard Space Flight Center. Several of the scientists there came to him independently and pleaded with him to train his students to work cooperatively. They complained that new Ph.D. scientists were coming to them lacking the skills and attitudes necessary for their highly collaborative working environment. Bill believes that his students need experiences that are as close as possible to doing real science in the real world. For him, that means both working cooperatively and collaboratively with a team and working with real, messy data—"the raw stuff."

He decided to apply his expertise as a meteorologist to create a learning environment in which students experience both these characteristics of science research and application. He has created a laboratory in the school in which he and his students use a weather satellite direct readout ground station to obtain raw satellite data from the receiving antenna on the roof of the school. Every three hours this receiving equipment brings pictures of the entire western hemisphere in both visible and infrared light, in quadrants. The work of accessing the satellite, saving images on a disk, calibrating the images, and analyzing the data requires extreme patience, attention to technical detail, and trial and error. His high school senior interns need a month just to learn to operate the equipment.

The projects they undertake require close cooperation among members of a team. For example, when Hurricane Hugo hit the U.S. mainland the students decided to undertake a study to try to understand why, in the face of contrary predictions, the hurricane went over the mountains into the Ohio Valley. The students worked as a research team, with Bill serving in the role of principal investigator. They used a variety of data sources for their investigation. Some went to the NOAA library to research the behavior of hurricanes, some were getting the 34,000 foot windspeed data from NOAA, some were getting ground data from the National Weather Service through the National Geographic Society's online "Weather Machine," and others were calibrating and analyzing the data they had downloaded from the geostationary orbiting satellite.

One of the students' current projects is to determine the "ground truth"-i.e., accuracy—of the temperature data received from the satellite by comparing it to ground-based and sea-based sources of the same temperature information. This requires the students to coordinate their efforts closely so that they access and collate the temperatures for the same places and times. They use a NOAA Remote Bulletin Board System to access the ground- and sea-based temperature data, while they get the satellite data directly from their receiving antenna. The infrared image contains coded information telling how to calibrate the images for temperature. It takes a knowledgeable person one hour to calibrate just one satellite image. Hence, the students must develop patience and learn to tolerate failure.

The typical class time period in school does not allow for the complex, time-dependent kind of work with raw data that Bill Krayer does with his small group of senior intern students. In his regular earth science classes he relies more on images that have already been downloaded, calibrated, and archived on disk. He typically uses these in demonstration mode to illustrate a point in his lecture. Occasionally he does get real-time data in the regular classroom, for example, if there is a front coming through. When timing permits, he likes to show the real-time satellite picture of a front coming through and then take the class outdoors to experience the front firsthand.

Bill himself has to overcome many obstacles and work under less than ideal circumstances in order to create these learning experiences for his students. It took him two years to get up to speed technically in the use of the equipment. The documentation for the computer software was full of errors and nearly impossible to understand. For getting data via telecommunications, he has only an old, slow modem in an inconveniently located room, and no dedicated telephone line. He has to conduct his special senior intern class during a "sixth period" for which he is not compensated. He is not provided with any preparation time, either, so all of the work of learning the technology and attempting to publish the students' work must be done at night and on weekends. Why does he do this? He enjoys the opportunity to employ his expertise in meteorology "to do some things that need to be done" in the schools—that is, provide students with opportunities to do real science.

Teaching for Understanding

Jim Minstrell, a high school physics teacher, says, "If the teacher can identify the particular concept or piece of information a student needs, the teacher can help make the learning process much more efficient for that student." We cannot help students develop scientific understanding without grasping the depth and tenacity of the students' preexisting conceptions about the world and how it works. In effective classrooms, teachers and students know that in order to understand the world the way the experts do, they need to talk about their naive theories (sometimes called "misconceptions") and test their theories against evidence. They realize that a qualitative understanding of core concepts is critical for organizing an intelligent, rational attack on a problem. Therefore they take time to understand core concepts in a qualitative way before they attempt to apply quantitative methods to solution of problems.

The teacher takes the time to help students uncover their incorrect notions. The teacher (or classmates) seek to create conflict between the student's misconception and the accepted scientific theory by asking some judicious questions that elicit a contradiction, or some obvious inconsistency between the student's beliefs and accepted scientific theory. In confronting the contradiction, the student begins to reconstruct knowledge. The teacher now plays the dual roles of guide to help the student through the process of reconstruction and of monitor to ensure that the student arrives at the desired goal.

Jim has been a leader in furthering our understanding of students' conceptions in physics. Thus, he views one of his main responsibilities as a teacher to be the diagnosis of each of his students' current conceptions in the area of physics being studied. Yet he does not have the time to interview each student individually. Furthermore, he wants his students to take responsibility for identifying their own conceptions. To assist the students in this process, he has created a set of HyperCard stacks (see Chapter 10) containing a library of problem situations designed to elicit the students' conceptions about those situations. The program then suggests to the student a particular learning experience such as an experiment that will help him or her move from the naive conception to a more expert understanding of the idea. Jim is now sharing these stacks with other teachers in his school and town, so that they can both learn from it and contribute further to the database.

Computational Science

Computational science is an emerging discipline that encompasses computational methods in various scientific and mathematical fields. Increasing numbers of secondary school teachers are becoming interested in teaching computational science, primarily because of a contest called Superquest in which student teams develop projects using supercomputers. Examples of recent winning Superquest project topics include:

- Optimization of traffic light cycles
- Architectural acoustic design of concert halls
- Testing the island biogeography model for species number in an ecosystem
- Inverse subsonic wing design
- Evolution of neural networks
- Galactic collisions

Although some people might imagine that such activities are only for the "gifted and talented" at high-tech magnet schools, these activities are also extremely valuable for more "ordinary" students. Sharon Carruth is a teacher at the J. O. Johnson High School in Huntsville, Alabama. The student population there is about 1,100—75 percent nonwhite and 25 percent white. It is typical for the students not to expect to go to college, and many have limited mathematics backgrounds.

During the 1987-88 school year, Sharon learned about the Superquest competition and thought there could be benefits to her students from participating. She began by coaching eight of her best students outside the regular school day. The students selected topics, identified problems to solve, and worked closely with engineers and research scientists as mentors. Sharon arranged these mentorships with scientists at the University of Alabama. The students were semifinalists in the competition. This close working relationship on an actual application resulted in the students finishing the year with a tremendous sense of accomplishment.

Based on this exciting and successful beginning, Sharon decided to offer the opportunity to the computer programming I class during the 1988-89 school year. The best projects were submitted to Superquest again and also made the semifinals. Based on these competitions she realized the benefits of such a program and in the spring of 1989 wrote a proposal seeking funding for a facility at Johnson to connect to the Alabama Supercomputer Network in order to allow students to follow through on their hard work and receive credit for a course in supercomputing.

Although she was not successful in securing funds for a facility, Sharon and thirteen other Alabama teachers were selected to participate in a pilot program for the training of high school teachers in computational science. The program was directed by the University of Alabama in Huntsville and funded through appropriations to the Alabama Commission on Higher Education. Johnson received a connection to the CRAY X-MP/24 through the efforts of the University of Alabama at Huntsville. Sharon developed the introduction to supercomputing course for Johnson based on competition guidelines and material covered by the teacher training course. Prerequisites are algebra II or teacher approval.

The course was implemented during the 1989-90 school year. Twenty-three students were enrolled whose backgrounds ranged from algebra II to A.P. calculus. The composition of the class was four white, nineteen nonwhite, eleven female, twelve male. Based on the success and enthusiasm of previous students for real applications and working with mentors, the course is project oriented. The languages covered are FORTRAN and BASIC. The approach to the material assumes the students have never had any programming and their math level is no higher than algebra I.

Sharon believes her approach builds confidence in students and develops the research, writing, communication, and programming skills they need for more complex projects. As students choose topics for projects their math and science background becomes more important but does not limit their choices; it only determines the level of difficulty for the student to overcome. Some of the best projects have come from algebra II students excited over the discovery of new mathematics with scientific applications that they were able to come to understand. The need for a better background in math and science is brought sharply to their attention as they realize that what appear to be simple problems require complex math and physics in order to determine a solution.

Their realization of this lack of knowledge combined with their desire to accomplish the task detailed in their project abstracts creates students with a strong desire to learn. All of Sharon's students except one completed the course by looking forward to pursuing a career in science, engineering, or computer science when originally only one or two even planned to attend college.

The supercomputing class had fifty-four students enrolled in the 1990-91 school year. The students ranged in background from unified geometry to A.P. calculus and in grade level from 9-12.

Putting It All Together: Voyage of the MIMI

Voyage of the MIMI is an outstanding set of educational materials that illustrates many of the themes of this chapter. The original Voyage of the MIMI is a dramatized story of a scientific expedition off the coast of New England to track, observe, and catalog whales. The crew included both scientists and teenagers. The second voyage is an adventure to Mexico to study the ancient Mayan civilization. One of the important features of the stories are "expeditions" in which crew members visit places such as research labs and museums to get more background on topics raised during the voyage.

The materials combine video, computer software, and print to present an integrated set of concepts in science, math, social studies, and language arts. For example, as the crew navigates the boat, there are opportunities for measurement, mapping, graphical representation, and astronomy. Software includes programs on maps and navigation, ecosystems, whales (which uses an MBL approach), "Mayan" math, and astronomy. The video is available on tapes or videodisc. There are also teacher guides, wall charts, audiotapes, and other related materials. The videos are closed-captioned in English and Spanish.

The Voyage of the MIMI materials were created by the Bank Street College of Education. They are available from Wings for Learning as well as other sources.

Summary

The main thrust of this chapter is that computers make it possible for students to learn science by actually doing it. Through the use of MBLs, students can collect and analyze data. Software tools such as databases, spreadsheets, and graphing programs allow data to be interpreted and manipulated. The use of video and videodisc helps students visualize scientific information. Simulation modeling can provide students with an understanding of scientific phenomena. Networks permit students to collaborate and share information.

The teachers discussed in this chapter tell some remarkable stories about what they and their students have been able to accomplish in the science classroom. In some cases the distinction between students and real scientists has become fuzzy. There can be little doubt that the use of technology can vastly improve the quality of science education at all levels. So why isn't everyone doing it?

Further information

A good source of information about the use of computers in science teaching are the *Journal of Research in Science Teaching* from NSTA and the *Journal of Computers in Mathematics and Science Teaching* published by the AACE (see address in Chapter 14). The two magazines published by the NSTA, *Science and Children* and *Science Teacher,* also contain articles about the use of computers in science teaching and software reviews. The newsletter published by TERC (see address in chapter 13) is also a good source of information about current developments in science education and technology.

Abruscato, J. (1986). *Children, Computers and Science Teaching*. Englewood Cliffs, NJ: Prentice-Hall.

Ellis, James. (Summer 1990). Preparing Science Teachers for the Information Age. *Journal of Computers in Mathematics and Science Teaching*, Vol 9(4), pp. 55-70.

National Science Teachers Association, 1742 Connecticut Ave. NW, Washington, D.C. 20009. (202) 328-5800.

Thornton, Ronald, & Sokoloff, David. (1991). Learning Motion Concepts Using Real-Time Microcomputer-Based Laboratory Tools. *American Journal of Physics*, 59(4), pp. 375-376.

Woerner, J., Rivers, R., & Vocknell, E. (1991). *The Computer in the Science Curriculum.* New York: McGraw-Hill.

Activities

- Obtain a copy of the videotape of the Kids Network from the National Geographic Society. Watch the video with some colleagues or classmates and create a list of the kinds of skills and knowledge you think students are learning in this project. What are some of the teaching challenges in this setting?

- Become familiar with the operation of particular MBL equipment and software. Create and test a lesson plan appropriate for the subject and grade you teach, using selected MBL probes.

- A considerable amount of research has been done concerning teaching and learning with MBL. Review the literature in this area and create a list of major findings concerning MBL use in science labs and classroom. How can you apply these findings in your teaching? If you have already created an MBL-based lesson plan, how would you revise it based on your review of the literature?

- Imagine that you have a supercomputer in your school. What kinds of student projects would you use it for? Could any of these projects be done on a personal computer?

- See if you can find teachers who have used the Voyage of the MIMI materials. How did it change their teaching approach? Did they find it a worthwhile experience? What problems did they encounter?

Chapter 7
Doing Mathematics

Of all the current reforms in education, perhaps none affects as many teachers in as many ways as the changes in what and how mathematics is taught. The National Council of Teachers of Mathematics, in its 1989 curriculum and evaluation standards, describes the following goals for students:

- Learning to value mathematics.
- Becoming confident in one's own ability.
- Becoming a mathematical problem solver.
- Learning to communicate mathematically.
- Learning to reason mathematically.

These goals, it is widely agreed, are not just for a small group of "mathematically talented" learners, but for *all* students.

The problem for most teachers is that achieving these goals means teaching in very different ways from how the teachers themselves were taught. As the NCTM standards state quite simply, "*What* a student learns depends to a great degree on *how* he or she has learned it." Rather than memorizing and practicing definitions and algorithms, students are now expected to construct their own mathematical understanding, to engage in mathematical discourse, and to take charge of their own learning.

© *John Colletti*

Teachers who adopt these reforms are finding they are *doing* mathematics, rather than just teaching the subject, and they are collaborating with fellow teachers in thinking about mathematics. They also must confront many deep issues concerning their roles as teachers, their own mathematical knowledge, their mathematical behavior, and their teaching behaviors. An integral part of these changes is the nature of the materials and technology tools the teachers use and how they use them. In this chapter we provide glimpses of these changing teachers and the ways in which they are using technology to support the changes.

Technology and Mathematics Education

Computers have been used in mathematics education for many years. Indeed, mathematics teachers were the first group to try computers in the classroom and were often the most enthusiastic users in a school. Some of the first computer-based teaching programs of twenty-five years ago were for arithmetic drill and practice, and this is still one of the most commonly used kinds of computer programs in education. When the BASIC programming language came into widespread use in the 1970s, it was very popular with mathematics teachers. For example, in 1979 David Ahl edited a book called *Computers in Mathematics: A Sourcebook of Ideas,* which consisted of hundreds of problems and solutions in BASIC. Although these programs were simple compared with the capabilities of today's software tools, they made it possible for teachers and students to take a "hands-on" approach to mathematics. For many, this provided the first opportunity to "do" mathematics instead of just talking or reading about it.

Given this legacy of computer use in education (not to mention calculators), it is not too surprising to find mathematics teachers on the "cutting edge" of technology use. This use of technology is driven by new developments in pedagogy and software tools that support the reforms being proposed by the NCTM. One development is that teachers and students are using tools that have been available for a long time (e.g., graphing programs, spreadsheets, LOGO) in new ways that emphasize critical thinking skills, collaborative learning, and visualization. In addition, there are many new software tools that take advantage of recent advances in computer capabilities. In the rest of this chapter we describe both types of developments and the variety of ways that teachers are making mathematics more interesting and relevant to their students through the use of technology.

Some Thoughts on Computers and Mathematics

Dr. David Moursund has been teaching about computers in education since 1963. He is a professor of education at the University of Oregon and a founder of the International Society for Technology in Education (ISTE). Here are some of his thoughts about computers and mathematics:

Both my father and mother were mathematics department faculty members at the University of Oregon. The combination of genetics, home environment, and our school system led me quickly and painlessly to a Ph.D. in mathematics. At one time I did mathematical research, adding to the pool of mathematical knowledge. Now I am a computer educator and I still enjoy mathematics.

With a computer, one can have software to graph, solve equations, and do algebraic manipulation. This sort of computer progress suggests possible changes in mathematics education. Both the calculator and the computer allow an increased separation of algorithmic processes from other aspects of knowing and doing mathematics. Algorithmic processes can be carried out by a machine—generally more rapidly than by a person assisted by pencil and paper.

It is difficult to appreciate the potential impact of computer-as-tool on mathematics. Our entire mathematics education system is built around a balance among the capabilities of paper and pencil, book, and human mind. The computer has certain characteristics of each of these. What will it be like to begin one's formal studies of math in kindergarten or the first grade seated in front of a very sophisticated computer? What does it mean to "know" mathematics when this knowing takes full advantage of the capabilities of the computer? If a computer can solve or help solve a particular category of problem, what do we want students to learn to do mentally, assisted by paper and pencil, or assisted by a computer?

My feeling is that the computer is a powerful enough change agent to move mathematics out of its current "local maximum" position. The risks are high . . . but the potentials are also high. What a great time to be a mathematics educator! And what a challenge to mathematics educators.

Source: From *High Tech, High Touch: A Computer Education Leadership Development Workshop,* published by the ISTE.

Manipulatives and the Computer

Manipulatives are physical objects such as blocks, pegboards, or rods that provide a physical and concrete basis for learning mathematics. They have been used in elementary math classrooms for many years to help children understand abstract ideas (and make learning more fun). The use of manipulatives is supported by Piagetian theory, which suggests that children in the concrete-operational learning stage cannot handle abstract concepts directly.

Computers can complement the traditional use of manipulatives. They can extend initial experiences gained with physical objects and bridge the gap to abstract concepts. Programs such as Gertrude's Secrets (The Learning Company) and Math Concepts (IBM Corp.) provide students with an unlimited supply of objects on the screen to work with. Elastic Lines (Sunburst) allows students to perform geoboard activities and Puzzle Tanks (Sunburst) lets students fill and empty containers. In Measurement, Time and Money (IBM), students can make different combinations of coins. In The Factory (Sunburst) students can assemble a "product" using a variety of movements and effects.

The use of the computer for manipulatives has practical advantages as well. Activities can be demonstrated more easily to a group of students using an LCD projector or large monitor. Many programs include score keeping, diagnostic, or student management capabilities that allow teachers to keep track of how students are doing. And software does not require any cleanup after the activity is over!

See Perl (1990) for further discussion of manipulatives and computers.

Spreadsheets

In Chapter 2 we introduced spreadsheets as a teacher tool. Spreadsheets can also play a major role in mathematics classes. Here are some examples of applications that teachers have used in their classes:

• Students create a spreadsheet template to calculate the profit and expenses of a business venture (e.g., a lemonade stand, car wash, etc.). Students have to make decisions about pricing, inventory, advertising, and wages. The class can be divided into competing groups that ultimately have to help each other. Graphing programs can be used to show sales statistics and analyze success factors. Certificates for sales awards can be made using desktop publishing software.

• Students use a spreadsheet to prepare a food and/or home budget for a month. Students need to be given guidelines for the items and costs to be included. Supermarket circulars can be used for food prices. Classified ads in a newspaper can be used to select jobs and salary. Appropriate amounts for savings, entertainment, and "luxury" items can be determined by percentages.

• Students create spreadsheets to solve algebra word problems. For example, find the number of nickels and quarters to make up $2.35. Students create columns for the number of nickels and quarters and the formula for the total amount. They can then vary the number of nickels and quarters until they get the desired total. Students can also be challenged to make up their own variations on the given problem.

• Students take a field trip to a local cemetery and record the names, dates of birth and death, sex, and any other information available. Have students input their data into a spreadsheet and calculate the average age of death and number of births/deaths by year. Graphs of the data can be used to help make conclusions about longevity. Historical information about local disasters, wars, or the economy can be used to interpret the data.

• Students are given values for equations to enter as data in spreadsheets and then create graphs. For example, provide data for x, y and a constant and ask students to study the effects of change of x on y (concept of slope). Provide data for exponential functions and ask students to examine the shape of the curves produced. Students can also make up their own data sets and equations.

• Students collect newspaper data on temperature or air quality for cities across the state or country over a series of weeks. They enter the data in spreadsheets and create graphs of the data to look for trends. The data can be related to discussions about pollution or weather.

As these examples illustrate, use of spreadsheets easily leads to cross-curriculum projects and cooperative learning activities. Integrated programs that include graphing and database capabilities are especially helpful in these kind of classroom applications.

For more details about the use of spreadsheets in mathematics, see Arganbright (1985), Verderber (1990), or Wood (1990). Many of the materials for integrated programs such as AppleWorks or Microsoft Works contain ideas for classroom applications of spreadsheets as well (see Chapter 2).

LOGO and Geometry

Computers have had an enormous impact on the teaching of geometry. With the availability of good graphing programs and visualization software (discussed later), teaching geometry has become more open-ended and exploratory than the traditional emphasis on memorizing theorems and proofs. This new approach is consistent with research finding that students pass through different levels of geometric thinking: visualization, analysis, and deduction.

The computer language LOGO has proved valuable in the teaching of geometry at the elementary school level (Clements & Battista, 1989). In particular, LOGO can:

- Help students move from empirical to logical thinking.
- Encourage students to make and test conjectures.
- Facilitate precision and exactness in geometric thinking.
- Encourage the development of autonomy in learning.
- Act as a mirror, reflecting the geometric thinking of students for teachers and themselves.

For example, LOGO activities can help children understand the concept of path and its relationship to two-dimensional shapes. Children form paths by walking, then using LOGO, and thus they can think of the program's actions as ones that they can perform. Studying the concept of a rectangle, students are initially able only to identify visually presented examples. Using LOGO, students can be asked to construct a sequence of commands (procedure) to draw a rectangle. In constructing a procedure for a rectangle, students must analyze the visual aspects of a rectangle and reflect on how its component parts are put together.

The fundamental characteristic of using LOGO in geometry classes is that students actively construct their own understanding of mathematics. They use a computer to create geometric shapes, change them, move them around, and combine them into new shapes. They discuss what they have done with each other and the teacher. In doing so, they progress to higher levels of geometric thinking.

For further discussion of LOGO, see Chapter 10.

Guided Inquiry and Technology

One of the major issues associated with the use of technology in the classroom is the need for new teaching/learning strategies. A group of researchers at the Education Development Center in Newton, Massachusetts conducted a year-long study of three high school math classes using a "guided inquiry" strategy in conjunction with the Geometric Supposer program. The study examined the nature of student learning and teacher experiences using the strategy and the software in geometry.

Here is how the researchers describe the purpose of the project, the nature of the teaching/learning process, and the overall results:

We argue that geometry instruction would be more effective if, rather than teaching definitions and theorems as givens and concentrating on proof, it were to give students an opportunity to experiment with geometric shapes and elements, to move from the particular to the general, and to make conjectures before grappling with proofs. We want to test the notion that by asking and enabling students to explore geometry, they will become more engaged in the subject matter, approach the task of devising proofs with more motivation and understanding, become more skilled at inductive and deductive reasoning, and ultimately learn more geometry.

In the pedagogy which we call guided inquiry, the teacher introduces content which is illuminated and modified in light of student inquiry and supplemented and complemented by the discussion of student findings. The teacher defines the focus of inquiry by posing a problem for the class. The students working in groups or two or three investigate the problem at the computer. These groups them join together as a class led by the teacher to share their findings and results and develop a collective understanding of the problem and issues at hand. The construction of knowledge is enriched and is enforced by a collaborative process among students and between students and teachers.

In this approach there is a significant shift in the teacher's role from what one normally sees in a high school mathematics class. In guided inquiry, the teacher is not the sole source of knowledge, direction or energy in the classroom. The teacher can shape the overall flow of the curriculum and the learning process, but on a class-to-class basis shares the control with the students. In short, to be successful in this guided inquiry approach requires a person who knows the subject matter, can function as a leader and manager of a community of learners, is flexible, and has time for planning and preparation throughout the year.

Students who used the Geometric Supposer in a guided inquiry approach developed and demonstrated a sensibility and some skills essential for creating mathematics. They learned as much geometry as the comparison group, they significantly outperformed the comparison group in their ability to develop generalizations, and they were equal to or somewhat better than the comparison group in their ability to devise informal arguments and traditional formal proofs. In addition to their mathematics learning, students gained new insights into what it means to be an active learner and to be a member of a community of learners.

Source: Yerushalmy, Chazan & Gordon (1990).

Visualization

Probably the most important capability that computers have introduced into mathematics teaching is improved visualization through the use of graph-

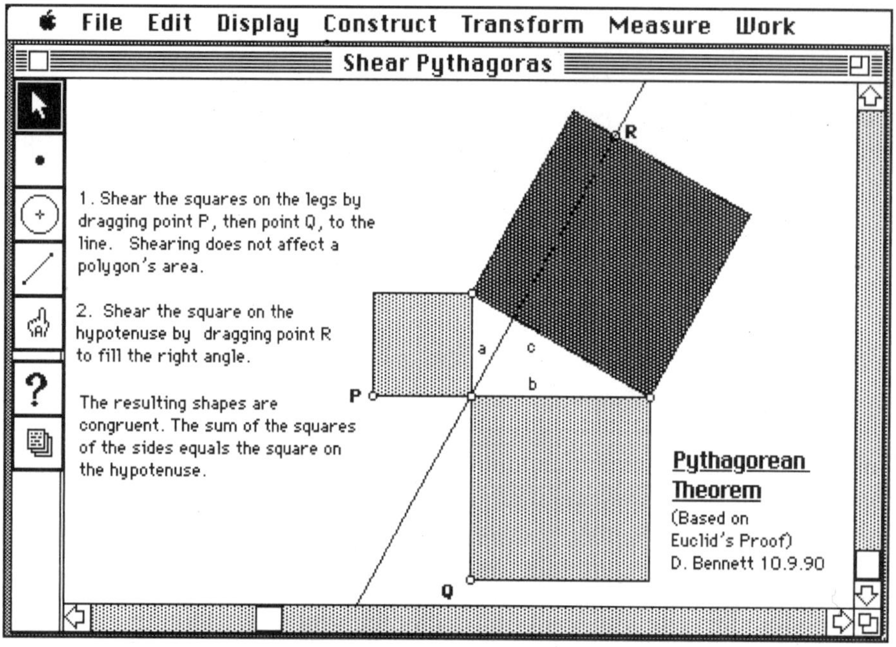

Figure 7-1 Graphics programs allow students to see the dynamics of mathematical relationships.

ing software. Mathematics teachers have always relied on graphs to help students understand the basic concepts of geometry, calculus, and algebra. However, drawings on the chalkboard, illustrations in textbooks, or student constructions on graph paper all suffer from the fact that they are *static*. Graphics programs allow the *dynamics* of mathematical relations and equations to be shown and examined (see Figure 7-1).

At the middle and high school level, programs such as Green Globs and the Geometry Supposer (Sunburst), the Geometer's Sketchpad (Key Curriculum Press), and GraphMaker/GraphWiz (William K. Bradford) are used extensively by both teachers and students. Teachers use these programs with an LCD panel to introduce new concepts to the class; students use them in class activities or when doing their homework.

In higher education, a relatively new category of software called mathematics processors has become popular. These programs (originally designed as tools for professional mathematicians and engineers) can solve equations, factor polynomials, do integration and differentiation, and plot results. Mathematica (Wolfram Research), Theorist (Prescience Corp), and MAPLE (Brooks/Cole) are examples of such programs. Mathematics instructors around the country report that the use of these programs is dramatically changing the way they teach and the nature of student learning.

For example, Ed Chandler, a math teacher at Paradise Valley Community College in Phoenix, Arizona feels that the traditional teaching methods used in calculus classes discourage many students from studying mathematics. The low rate of completion in calculus courses has prompted instructors at his institution to explore alternative methods. Ed is trying to revamp his teaching through the use of a variety of different software, especially mathematics processors. He hopes that use of these programs will help students focus on concepts instead of routine calculations and ultimately make the study of mathematics more interesting.

Bill Davis, a professor at Ohio State University, believes that most students learn to manipulate numbers mechanically but gain no understanding of the meanings that lie behind the manipulations or how these can be applied to the solution of real-world problems. Many courses, he says, don't require students to do anything a calculator can't do. In his courses he focuses on getting students to use Mathematica to solve real problems. The program relieves students from worrying about the routine calculations and gives them a chance to understand what calculus is all about.

The use of math programs in the classroom presents some problems for teachers. Adding computers to a course normally requires substantial changes to the curriculum and teaching methods. A lot of time is needed to develop new lesson plans and class activities—time often taken from evenings and weekends. Additional time is required to learn how to use the mathematics software itself. Another consideration is whether extensive reliance on mathematics software produces students who don't know how to do computations manually. Many teachers worry that if students become completely dependent on computers to perform routine calculations, they won't know if the results they get are reasonable. Finally, some math teachers find they spend too much of their time dealing with computers instead of mathematics.

Computer-Intensive Algebra: Mathematical Models

In 1985 a group of mathematics educators at the University of Maryland (led by James Fey) and Pennsylvania State University (led by Kathleen Heid) proposed a new approach to elementary algebra that would exploit the use of computers as learning and problem-solving tools. Over the next six years a team of researchers, curriculum developers, and classroom teachers developed and field tested software and materials for teaching algebra to middle school students. The result of these efforts is a set of teaching/learning materials that supports the computer-intensive algebra class.

The materials provide students with an opportunity to explore mathematics in real-world situations though the development and evaluation of mathematical models. Working with these models, students develop representations of data, explore relevant questions, and formulate predictions. To reason about important applied problems, students use fundamental mathematical ideas and methods. Students learn properties of variables, functions, relations, and systems as they investigate realistic questions. Computers and calculators facilitate students' explorations by providing access to numerical, graphical, and symbolic representations of mathematical ideas.

The different goals of the computer-intensive algebra approach result in different classroom activities. There is no longer a typical daily routine consisting of homework review, examples of new problem types, and seatwork until the bell rings. Instead, classroom activities vary from whole group discussion to computer exploration to data collection. Students usually work in pairs at the computers and in small groups during data-gathering activities.

Teachers must serve as catalysts and facilitators of learning during whole class discussion and while interacting with pairs of students in the laboratory setting. Students begin to take on more responsibility for assessing their own learning. Since the curriculum emphasizes conceptual learning and complex problem solving, students must adopt more reflective habits and sustain their attention for longer times. The major role of mathematical modeling implies that students must make notes about the patterns they observe in their computer explorations and write reports on the results of their problem solving. The open-ended nature of the questions posed requires both teachers and students to accept the existence of a variety of correct responses.

The computer-intensive algebra materials involve a student text, teaching guide, sample tests/answers, and software for MS-DOS computers. The materials are available from the Office of Technology Liaison, Room 2114 Lee Building, University of Maryland, College Park, MD 20742.

Computer Animation, Video and Videodisc

One aspect of technology that offers considerable promise for mathematics instruction is computer animation. Since many of the principles to be learned involve dynamic components, animated sequences can demonstrate these concepts much better than static diagrams or graphs. Animation can be interactive or captured on videotape or videodisc.

For example, Project Mathematics!, headed by Tom Apostol, professor of Mathematics at California Institute of Technology, has developed a series of videotapes on the Pythagorean theorem, pi, and similiarity that use computer animation to present these topics in a stimulating and effective manner. The tapes and materials are distributed in partnership with the departments of education in thirty-two states as well as the NCTM.

Another interesting use of video is the TapeMeasure project conducted by Andee Rubin at the Technical Education Research Center in Cambridge,

Massachusetts. TapeMeasure is a program that allows students to record measurements on videotape. They can choose particular frames to measure and advance the tape a frame at a time. The program includes a ruler, stopwatch, and protractor as well as "mark-up" tools that students use to prepare frames for measurement. Students can use the program to analyze data collected in video format. For example, one class of junior high school students investigated the variables that affect running speed. They designed a variety of running experiments, videotaped the results using themselves as subjects, and then used TapeMeasure to analyze the data.

Researchers at Vanderbilt University have a number of projects that involve interactive videodisc and mathematics education. The Adventures of Jasper Woodbury, developed by the Learning Technology Center, presents a series of adventures that require various kinds of mathematical problem solving. Students watch stories that are rich in detail and have to formulate solutions based upon the details provided. The Teaching and Learning department of has developed a set of videodiscs and accompanying HyperCard stacks that can be used to demonstrate teaching methods for elementary mathematics. The video sequences show actual mathematics classes being taught and and provide examples of specific teaching techniques and topics (see Goldman & Barron, 1990).

Additional discussion of animation and video is provided in Chapter 11.

Summary

As this chapter has illustrated, computers are being used in many different ways in mathematics classrooms. However, one consistent theme runs through all of these applications—the notion of active involvement by students.

Whether the activity is LOGO use by elementary students, use of spreadsheets or graphing programs in high school, or use of mathematics processors at the college level, the primary function of the computer is to provide students with a tool that lets them explore or experiment with mathematical concepts.

A second theme of this chapter is that the use of technology encourages the use of new teaching and learning strategies. Most computer learning activities are done in pairs or small groups and involve a considerable amount of discussion among students and between students and teacher. A much more open-ended teaching style is involved and student learning is more self-directed. Traditional forms of evaluation (e.g., multiple choice tests) are not very appropriate methods of assessment for computer activities; self/peer evaluation, written reports, and demonstration projects make more sense.

The way computers are now being used in mathematics classrooms supports new ideas about how mathematics should be taught. At the same time, research on computer use in mathematics is providing new ideas about how students learn and about effective teaching practices.

Further Information

Discussions of software for K-12 mathematics education can be found in Dickey (1990) and Flake (1990). Research studies are reported in Charles & Silver (1989) and Grouws & Cooney (1988) as well as the *Journal of Computers in Mathematics and Science Teaching* and *Journal for Research in Mathematics Education.*

References

Ahl, D. (1979). *Computers in Mathematics: A Sourcebook of Ideas.* Morristown, NJ: Creative Computing Press.

Arganbright, D. (1985). *Mathematical Applications of Electronic Spreadsheets.* New York: McGraw-Hill.

Charles, R., & Silver, E. (1989). *The Teaching and Assessing of Mathematical Problem Solving.* Hillsdale, NJ: Erlbaum.

Clements, D., & Battista, M. (1989). Learning of geometric concepts in a LOGO environment. *Journal for Research in Mathematics Education, 20,* pp 450-467.

Dickey, E. (Summer 1990). Mathematics software for young children. *Journal of Computing in Childhood Education,* Vol 1*(4)*,pp. 3-13

Fey, J. T. (1984). *Computers and Mathematics: The Impact in Secondary School Curriculum.* Reston, VA: National Council of Teachers of Mathematics.

Flake, J. (1990). *Computer-Intensive Middle and Secondary Mathematics Education.* Belmont, CA: Wadsworth.

Goldman, E., & Barron, L. (1990). Using Hypermedia to Improve the Preparation of Elementary Mathematics Teachers. *Journal of Teacher Education, 41(3),* pp 21-31.

Gray, T., & Glynn, J. (1991). *Exploring Mathematics with Mathematica*. Reading, MA: Addison-Wesley.

Grouws, D. & Cooney, T. J. (1988). *Perspectives on Research on Effective Mathematics Teaching*. Hillsdale, NJ: Erlbaum.

National Council of Teachers of Mathematics. 1906 Association Dr., Reston, VA 22091. (703) 620-9840.

Perl, T. (March 1990). Manipulatives and the Computer: A Powerful Partnership for Learners of All Ages. *Classroom Computer Learning*, pp 20-29.

Project Mathematics! Caltech Bookstore, 1-51 Caltech, Pasadena, CA 91125. (818) 356-6161.

Verderber, N. (Spring 1990). Spreadsheets and Problem Solving with AppleWorks in Mathematics Teaching. *Journal of Computers in Mathematics and Science Teaching, (9)3*, pp 45-51.

Wood, J. (Spring 1990). Utilizing the Spreadsheet and Charting Capability of Microsoft Works in the Mathematics Classroom. *Journal of Computers in Mathematics and Science Teaching, (9)3*, pp 65-71.

Yerushalmy, M., Chazan, D., & Gordon, M. (1990). *Guided inquiry and technology*. Center for Learning Technology, Report 90-8. Education Development Center, Newton, MA 02160. (617) 969-7100.

Activities

- If you are an elementary school teacher and you use manipulatives in your teaching, obtain and review some of the programs discussed in this chapter. Modify a number of your existing lesson plans to include computer activities and try them. How did they change your teaching methods? How did they change student behavior?

- A considerable amount of research has been done concerning teaching and learning with LOGO in mathematics. Review at least ten articles/books on this subject and create a list of major findings. How can you apply these findings in your teaching? If you have already created a LOGO-based lesson plan, how would you revise it based on your review of the literature?

- Review your lesson plans and look for opportunities for using spreadsheets. Develop some new lessons involving their use and try them. Do you think students are learning something new when they use spreadsheets? Are they learning differently?

- Identify a topic that you have difficulty teaching or one that students always have trouble with. Think of some new ways you could teach this topic, emphasizing visualization of concepts and procedures. Develop a new lesson plan that involves the use of graphing software and hands-on activities.

Chapter 8
Places, People, and Cultures

Social studies covers history, geography, culture, government, and economics. The purpose of teaching social studies is to help students understand their past and their present and, hopefully, to create active citizens who will shape their own future.

For decades the primary tool used in the social studies classroom has been the textbook. Students have often been passive recipients of information. With new technologies, the teacher's role can be the facilitator of the learning process. The student becomes an active decision maker using new tools to gather information, organize and analyze it, and communicate it to a wide variety of audiences.

The teachers profiled in this chapter are inventing new and more powerful ways to help their students become careful decision makers, critical thinkers, preservationists of their culture, and shapers of their communities. Many of these teachers have extended their classrooms to make use of resources within their communities. They have also assisted their students in preparing newsletters, brochures, reports, and videos which can have wider dissemination to audiences in their community and even around the world. The technological tools used by these teachers include online databases, spreadsheets, word processors, interactive video, and telecommunications networks.

Although initially the impact of technology on social studies may have to do with the amount of information available (e.g., visual libraries on interactive videodisc or data on CD-ROM), the real challenge will be to focus on students intellectual development and their use of information to further their social participation skills. In order to meet this goal, students will need to collaborate on teams with other students as they work with information to set goals and to create projects that will be of wider use to others.

Equally important is the role that the social studies classroom plays in helping children to determine their own values and their role in civic participation. The ethical dilemmas of our past and present—slavery, Watergate, the savings and loan crisis—are topics of discussion and evaluation in the social studies classroom. Teachers assist children in understanding and preserving their own culture and discovering ways to integrate it into the curriculum.

Data Collection and Analysis

Data collection and analysis is a fundamental component of social studies. Many teachers have found that computers can be a wonderful focal point for such activities. Phil Jackson, a teacher in the Los Angeles Unified School District, wanted his students to learn how to use data analysis and management techniques in social studies. Phil assigned his students the task of interviewing people about their TV-watching habits. Students collected information on the number of hours watched per week, the most frequently watched shows, and the respondent's age. Then they labeled the categories in their database record format and entered their data. Next, Phil gave the students a problem to solve using their databases. For example, an advertising agent wants to know what TV show is watched by most people in order to place a commercial for a product.

Phil Jackson believes it's important to provide structured exercises and problems for his students when they're in the introductory stages of learning new skills. Their databases are quite small and contain only four items per record. In this way, he and the students stay focused on the original objectives: developing skill in interviewing and analyzing survey data. After all the students have achieved the initial objectives, those who are interested can then pursue projects that are more original and creative.

Most Livable Places

My name is Kathleen Smith and I teach eighth grade at Franklin Middle School in Champaign, Illinois. It is my class that will be trying to put together a survey of livability questions, and sending out the survey and compiling the results for the Most Livable Places for Kids Project . . . I think the project offers not only a good tool for teaching problem-solving techniques, data collection, and statistics, but can also be a valuable learning experience for the kids about the things that make different parts of this large country unique. Ultimately we hope to learn a good deal about the different places we live when we publish our Livability Index Ranking next spring.

Teachers like Kathleen Smith are developing a new approach to the teaching of social studies. Her focus is to help children connect their knowledge and skills to the world of their experience. By collaborating with other students around the world to discover "The Most Livable Places for Kids," her children learn to think "globally" about their world. Information and communication technologies dramatically change the way we access and share ideas.

Kathleen is helping her students to learn how to formulate questions that may be of interest to other students. She is teaching critical skills in data collection, analysis, and synthesis. And she is providing her students with an opportunity to collaborate in their work with children from around the world. In short, she is developing civic participation skills that will be useful to her students in the Information Age.

Simulations

For many educators, such as Don Rawitch, their first entree into the world of technology and social studies is with a simulation. Don created *Oregon Trail*, a simulation of the trip across the Oregon Trail distributed by the Minnesota Education Computing Consortium (MECC). Don's intention was to create a game that would make the classroom come alive for his students. The computer offered the possibility of "what if" decisions. Don created this game while a high school teacher working on his dissertation. He later went on to a career in the world of educational computing and currently serves as vice president for product development at Jostens Learning Corporation. Oregon Trail has become one of the most well-known educational programs.

Another simulation game, *SimCity*, (marketed by Brøderbund Software) has been used by Lori Martinez, a computer teacher, to provide students with firsthand experience in urban planning. This simulation enables students to design, build, and manage the city of their dreams. They can select one of eight scenarios. Each scenario focuses on a city that is either the victim of horrible planning or about to be the victim of a natural disaster. Timing and strategy determine the student's capabilities as mayor of these cities.

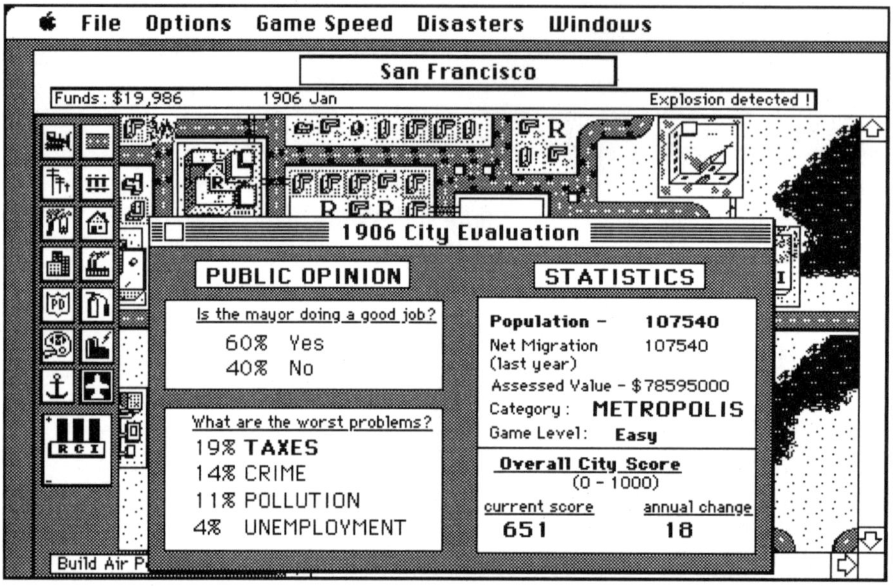

Figure 8-1 San Francisco scenario from SimCity (Brøderbund Software)

Students are able to test their plans and ideas as they watch the city grow or change (for example, see Figure 8-1). The program provides graphs that plot statistics such as projected population growth or crime rates as well as an evaluation rating of current performance. The success of the city is based on the types of decisions the students make in terms of services, transportation, zoning, power plants, tax rates, etc. They can build homes, hospitals, churches, stores, and factories in various city zones. Although SimCity was primarily intended as a game, it can be a very useful learning tool for social studies classrooms.

Phil Nelson, a teacher at Price School in northern Iowa, developed his own simulation for his high school economics class. The program, called *Wheels and Deals*, teaches students how to analyze the comparative cost of different automobiles and interest rates. In addition, it simulates the generation of auto insurance premiums and the decision-making by a loan officer on whether a student qualifies for an auto loan. Students gather information from auto dealers and lending agencies regarding prices, interest rates, and so forth. Then they use the simulation to see the effects of their choices on things such as monthly payments, total amount of interest paid over the life of the loan, and cost of the insurance.

Phil finds the computer useful not only as a tool for storing and analyzing data or performing simulations, but also as a tutor. Before he had computers in his classroom, he used to spend five days presenting concepts and examples of supply and demand on the chalkboard, tediously drawing graphs by hand. When he started working with computers, he designed and programmed a tutorial called Marketplace that teaches these concepts and principles and shows the examples in color graphs.

With this program, students can learn in three days the same material previously covered in five. More importantly, they have the opportunity to see many more graphic examples of supply and demand cases that illustrate the principles in consumer applications. Often Phil uses the computer-generated graphs as part of his lectures, in much the same manner as he formerly used the chalkboard.

Decisions, Decisions

Tom Snyder Productions has won much praise from teachers for innovative software that is highly effective in the classroom. One popular series of programs for social studies is called *Decisions, Decisions*. The programs encourage students to think critically about what they read, to make connections, and to anticipate the consequences of their decisions. They are based on a teaching model that involves group discussion and debate. The programs help students formulate their choices, provide multiple perspectives, and present the consequences of choices made.

Decisions, Decisions programs are available for the following topics:

- Colonization: exploring the New World
- Revolutionary wars: choosing sides
- Immigration: maintaining the open door
- Urbanization: the growth of cities
- Foreign policy: the burdens of world power
- Television: the study of media ethics
- The budget process: a question of balance
- On the campaign trail: issues and image
- The environment: science and politics of a cleaner world

Visual Libraries

Many aspects of social studies are visual in nature. Accordingly, the use of audiovisual media has always played an important role in social studies classrooms. However, this equipment is often unreliable and requires a lot of time to set up. Videocassette, videodisc, and CD-ROM players are much easier to use and offer many new and exciting possibilities in terms of student use and interaction.

Sandy Cheiten, a social studies teacher in New York City, now develops lesson plans to accompany the ABC News interactive videodisc series (distributed by Optical Data Corp). She learned that ABC News Interactive planned to create a videodisc that would have actual film of the civil rights movement while she was teaching and got involved in the development of the videodisc. She now helps teachers around the United States integrate interactive video into their social studies classrooms. ABC News also has videodiscs on Japan, the San Francisco earthquake, the Arab-Israeli conflict, and the AIDS epidemic. The first stage of use for teachers is using the videodisc as a browsing library; the second stage involves getting the students into the role of information producers. Students cut and paste sequences from the videodisc to prepare their own video documentary.

Magdalena Fittoria is a teacher in East Palo Alto, California, a disadvantaged community surrounded by considerably more affluent means. Ninety-nine percent of the students in her school are minorities. She is developing a project in which students will create multimedia videotape programs. This means the students will be able to edit videotapes and combine sequences to add title frames, and produce a new documentary. The programs will be on topics such as the local environment and community development issues. Students will conduct research, interview local community members, analyze local media reports, discuss their findings, and organize their thoughts into text, graphics, video, and sound formats.

Linking Children to Their Culture

Kathleen Duplantier's vision was to create an environment in which her children could create a curriculum focusing on the folklife of Abita Springs, Louisiana. Her students use Hypercard (see Chapter 10) to document their culture. (See Figure 8-2) They interview members of the school and the community to hear their stories about early life in Louisiana.

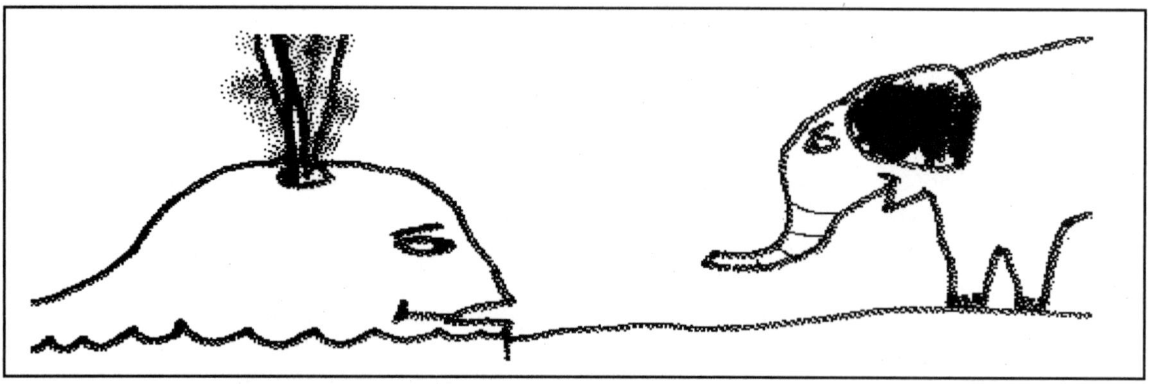

Figure 8-2 Student drawing from Folklife Stack.

The Hypertext Folklife Program is one year old. We received the computers about this time last year. In July, I was unpacking box after box and getting very nervous about what lay ahead of me. I am very fortunate to be at a school with an excellent faculty, so I was not at all worried about their ability to do this project. It was the technical expertise that none of us had that had me the most worried. My husband and a friend of his were our support on the technical stuff. I can't tell you how many mornings Steve came to school at 7:00 A.M. to help me figure out something else. I am still learning. The folklife part of the program just fell into place . . . as though some higher entity had that all arranged somewhere else. I really was lucky with the guests and the riches that arrived at our school.

The focus of my program is to collect information from the rich culturally diverse population and compile a Hypertext encyclopedia of the region. Abita Springs is above New Orleans and was settled by Native Americans, Afro-Americans, French, Germans, English, Italians, and Hungarians. At the elementary level, the school year is divided into cultures. The whole-language approach is used with the cultures as the themes. All the performance, art, and some of the music programs use the information from that culture. The writing assignments, of course, flow from the program. Some social studies and literature were woven into the program last year. More will be part of the program this year. There have been some exciting changes happening within the classrooms with the program and we anticipate more changes this year. At the junior high level, the students' focus was on foodways (easy to accomplish in Louisiana where everyone has foodway information). This has branched and will focus on hunting and fishing folkways this year. They have just finished an alligator stack with recipes and instructions on how to catch one.

A teacher-centered and -directed staff development program is the most recent result. I am presently trying to get this funded. The teachers have worked long and hard on making this project work, and I need to try to get some compensation for them. They were given permission to take the computers home this summer and I suspect that the technical skills will have increased tremendously by the time school starts. We are planning regular staff development time next year to focus on the goals of the program. I won't tell you what kind of budget we Louisiana teachers have for staff development! As I travel around, I realize that this is the one area that we need most and is ignored.

I have finally decided that this might be a life long project that might never end and I need to appreciate where we are now. I have certainly had some wonderfully gratifying days over this past year and the teachers and students have had some momentous moments. It has opened door after door for me personally and for the school. We have received two other (minor) grants, and we hope to try for other grants. The community is behind us 100 percent and the parents love it.

Collaboration and Cultural Exchange

A common theme for social studies teachers is to help children develop an understanding and appreciation of their own culture. With technology, teachers can find new ways of collaborating with children and other teachers and can help children learn about the culture of other places.

Classroom activities need to emphasis collaboration and teamwork. An approach that the authors integrated into their Scholastic PFS software for social studies involves five roles: team leader, information manager, researcher, editor, and public affairs person. Students work on projects such as building a local history of their community, using technology to support their work. The team leader organizes the activities of the group. The information manager uses the computer technology to collate the ideas of the group. The researchers collect the information from a variety of sources. The editor works with the material provided by the researchers and makes sure the finished product is cohesive and readable. The public affairs member of the team publicizes the ideas of the group.

Here are two examples of teachers who are using the Apple Global Education (AGE) network to help their students exchange information about the culture and lifestyle of others.

Georgia Ward, a teacher at Western High School in Louisville, Kentucky, uses the AGE network to try to find another teacher and class who will exchange letters in French.

I am a teacher of French and English in a secondary school, grades nine through twelve. My students range in age from fourteen to eighteen years.

Most of my French students are studying French for the first time. Several of them go on to study French for a second year, and a few of them will continue their study into a third, and perhaps a fourth year.

With the AGE program, I want my students to be able to communicate in French and English with students of French-speaking countries and to have a cultural exchange with them.

With the AT&T Long Distance Learning Network, teachers and students can participate in an "learning circle" with students around the world. Margaret Riel, an educator who pioneered this program, has created eight curriculum project outlines for the students and teachers. Each group selects a curriculum project. There are two in the area of social studies: People and Places and Social Problems. The teachers and students collaborate on a series of projects over the semester. Students produce a product that is the result of their collaboration. One example of the work produced by a learning circle is a series of pamphlets describing the communities of the children in the learning circle. (See chapter 5 for more about networks.)

Creating Wider Audiences

Linda Borders, an art instructor at Western High School in Louisville, Kentucky, is interested in finding wider audiences for the work of her students. She has posted a message on the Apple Global Education network to share the artwork of her students. She hopes to publish the students' work.

I am interested in sharing the artwork of my students with the artwork of their peers in other geographical locations. Black and white work and line artwork done with pen and ink, pencil, markers, etc. are suitable for the scanner. The artwork must also be able to fit on the scanner. The artwork can be exchanged, then printed and put on exhibit. We will be able to put this exhibit on display at the old Jefferson County Courthouse in Louisville, Kentucky.

If Linda Borders is able to implement her plan, she will have her children producing materials that are created collaboratively with children from around the world. And her children will share the results of their work with a wider audience—the local community of Louisville, Kentucky. Her students will be bringing a "global art exhibit" home. (See Chapter 11 for more about computers and art.)

Gaining Perspective on World Events

Social studies teachers have traditionally studied current events with their students. Typically, this is accomplished by having students read *Time* magazine and the newspaper, or watch the evening news. When children begin to use electronic networks they can have "immediate access" to information such as UPI or AP News.

But the next step is for the teacher to help children interpret world events from a variety of perspectives. Liz Cosgrove describes how this happened with her class last year:

I am a teacher of geography and history at a small school in Louisville, Kentucky. My students are fourteen to eighteen years old. The school has been established for students with behavior problems. These students are sent to us for difficulties they are having in other schools. Also we get children referred to us by the courts. These students need special motivation to come to school and to learn.

Last year I used the Apple Global Education network with these students very effectively. They wrote letters to students in Europe about the end of the Communist governments in Eastern Europe and on drug use in the U.S.

This year I would like to establish a correspondence with several schools around the world to develop a discussion of world events and issues which would affect these students in years to come. The format can be decided on when we have written to each other.

Jamie J. McMillin is an instructor in social sciences at J. Graham Brown School in Louisville, Kentucky:

Nineteen years of teaching have taught me to always delight in the unexpected from my students. Eighteen of those years have been experienced in the very unique Brown School. The school incorporates grades one through twelve and has about 650 students. It is the only public school of its kind in our city, therefore we would like to talk with all levels.

My interest is to create a network of students and schools determined to explore the possibilities of peace between nations of the world. I want to do this symbolically and verbally. To symbolize the effort, an exchange of nation flags between the students of my school and your school would take place. To verbalize the effort, a regular exchange of thoughts, impressions and reactions to world events and student ideas would begin with our first letters. We will publish world views of peace by students twice a year. Please respond to your future! Let's talk!

Here is one more example from the West Tisbury School on Martha's Vineyard in Massachusetts:

Dear Teachers and Students,

We feel that the unification of Germany is a significant event! As such, we would like to hear your opinions on what is happening. We realize that this is rather late, however, we would appreciate your responses today (if possible). We will collate the results and share them with all of you.

1. How do you think the unification of Germany will affect the people of Bonn and Berlin?

2. How do you feel this will affect the status of German women?

3. How do you feel this will affect the rest of Europe and other countries in the world?

4. What historic event in your history is comparable to the unification of Germany?
5. Will East and West Germany benefit equally from the unification? Why?
6. How will the world be affected by this historic event?
Thank you for your quick responses.

Sincerely,
Ginny and the students in West Tisbury.

Summary

Technology can help social studies teachers bring the world into their classroom and vice-versa. Through the use of simulations and visual libraries, computers and videodiscs can offer rich learning opportunities for students. Technology can help students discover their own culture and better understand the culture of others. It can help students achieve global perspectives and create a wider audience for their activities. For teachers, it makes the teaching of social studies exciting, challenging, and fun.

Further Information

In addition to the books by Abelson (1983), Braun (1986), Rooze & Northup (1989) and Walstad et al. (1986), there are a number of journals that focus on the use of computers in social science education. In addition, *Social Education*, the journal of the NCSS, regularly includes software reviews.

Abelson, R. B. (1983). *Using Microcomputers in the Social Studies Classroom.* Boulder, CO: Social Science Education Consortium. (303) 492-8154.

Braun, J. A. (1986). *Microcomputers and the Social Studies: A Reference Guide.* New York: Garland Publishing.

Brøderbund Software, P.O. Box 12947, San Rafael, CA.94903 (800) 521-6263.

History Microcomputer Review. Dept. of History. Pittsburg State University, Pittsburg, KS 66762. (316) 231-7000.

Hunter, M., & Furlong, M. *Scholastic PFS: Curriculum Data Bases for U.S. History/Government.* Available from Scholastic Software, P.O. Box 7502, Jefferson City, MO 65102. (800) 541-5513.

MECC, 3490 Lexington Ave. N., St. Paul, MN 55126. (612) 481-3500.

National Council for Social Studies, 3501 Newark St., NW, Washington, DC 20016. (202) 996-7840.

Rooze, G. E., & Northup, T. (1989). *Computers, Thinking and Social Studies.* Englewood, CO: Libraries Unlimited.

Social Science Computer Review. Duke University Press, 6697 College Station, Durham, NC 27708. (919) 684-2173.

Tom Snyder Productions, 90 Sherman St. Cambridge, MA 02140. (800) 342-0236.

Walstad, W., Hallows, K. S., & Ross, D. (1986). *Annotated Catalog of Microcomputer Software in Economics.* New York: Joint Council on Economic Education. (212) 685-5499.

Activities

- Use a database program to create a local history or government template for your community.

- Go online on CompuServe, Delphi, or America Online and access the AP or UPI newsline to research a current issue for your class. Participate in a forum discussion on a topic of current events.

- Create a project in which your students create a guide to your community. Use a computer and a scanner to record photographs of the community in 1920, 1940, 1960, 1980, and today. Use a desktop publishing program to print the final version. Distribute it to other groups in your community.

- Initiate a project with students in another cultural group (in your city or around the world). Create a project idea and then share the work—focusing on the problem, collecting the data, sharing the results, producing the final product.

- Develop a database of software, videodiscs, and CD-ROMs for use in a social studies classroom.

We live in a world that is increasingly multicultural. People travel extensively, the media constantly provide news from around the globe, and most countries are made up of a diverse range of ethnic groups.

These facts make language learning an important educational activity. On one hand, students who already speak English want to learn other languages so they can interact with people from foreign countries. On the other hand, students from other countries and immigrants want to learn English so they can take advantage of our educational system. Part of learning a new language is an understanding of the culture that underlies it. Computers can be helpful in many aspects of language learning, especially when teamed up with videodiscs and CD-ROM.

Chapter 9
Citizens of the World

Making Cross-Cultural Connections

Many projects have used computer networking to link students around the world. In these projects, students introduce themselves, answer questions, and share stories—learning about each other's culture in the process. Here are descriptions of some of these projects:

• Project De Orilla a Orilla was intended to improve student skills in writing Spanish and understanding of Hispanic culture. The project began by linking Puerto Rican students in the U.S. with students in Puerto Rico but eventually was extended to schools in Argentina and Canada. Students created newspapers based on the stories provided by "foreign correspondents" at other network sites.

• The Computer Chronicles project used the AT&T Long Distance Learning Network (LDLN) to create newspapers based on stories provided by students at sites all over the world. Each site selected the stories that interested it most and assembled its own issue of the Chronicles. Many newspapers focused on themes of global significance such as pollution, poverty, or peace.

• The Apple Global Education (AGE) project sponsored by Apple Computer and using AppleLink connects hundreds of schools throughout the world. The basic theme of the project is "to connect students of the world together." AGE provides lists of project ideas and a curriculum folder to help schools find partners for collaboration on the network. Projects include weather data collections, science problem solving, pollution and social issues, and comparisons of age/grade levels in different countries.

• The World 2000 project connects high school students in Juneau, Alaska, with their counterparts in Moscow. Teachers and students use electronic mail and computer conferences to share their experiences and research findings about global health issues. Their goal is to develop a collective vision of the world's health in the year 2000. The project expands the traditional learning environment as students come to see themselves as global citizens, capable of collaborating with people in other countries to address complex issues using telecommunications technologies.

See Chapter 5 for more discussion and examples of these and other networks.

Bilingual Education

Bilingual education represents an interesting link between teaching language arts (discussed in Chapter 3) and foreign language studies. The goal of bilingual education is to teach students to communicate in both English and their native language. In a sense, English is a foreign language that bilingual students must learn. English as a Second Language (ESL) programs try to make it easier for such students to attain sufficient English proficiency to do well in school.

One problem for bilingual students is that they are often perceived by English-speaking classmates as "stupid" or "slow learners" because of their language difficulties. One interesting way to change this perception is to have the class participate in a telecommunicatons project with students in another country that involves the sending and receiving of electronic messages in foreign languages. The bilingual students can then act as translators and become valuable members of the class.

At White Plains High School in New York, computers play a key role in the ESL program. Students are encouraged to celebrate their cultural heritage and family backgrounds as they learn English. Students use tape recorders to conduct family interviews and then transform the oral reports into written stories using word processing. They then review one another's work and revise their work based on the suggestions of their peers. Coordinator Kathy Rehfield-Pelless says that using a word processor enhances language learning: "Because of the fluidity and flexibility of writing on a word processor, students come to view speaking and writing in English as a process which they are constantly experiencing, editing, and reworking." Students can illustrate their written stories using graphics software. Publishing the histories in the student newspaper gives the entire student body a better understanding of other cultures and provides source materials for foreign language classes.

Software for Language Learning

There are many programs available that you can use to help your students learn a foreign language. Most of these programs are drills or games that focus on vocabulary or verb conjugation. Some of the programs include audio capabilities that allow the computer to pronounce words or sentences. The spoken words may be digitally recorded and stored on the disk or the program may synthesize the speech as needed. You can also buy authoring tools (see Chapter 10) that let you create your own drills or tutorials for foreign language teaching. For example, the *MacLang* program for the Macintosh (distributed by Intellimation) lets you create lessons in the following formats: drills, fill-in-the-blanks, multiple choice, and scrambled sentences. The program includes the alphabets for ten different languages, provides automatic scoring, allows branching, and can be used with Tandberg tape recorders or videodisc players.

In addition to drill and tutorial programs, many types of writing utilities (see Chapter 2) such as spelling and grammar checkers can also be useful in foreign language or ESL classes. A number of companies produce versions of these programs in multiple languages. Teachers and students can use these programs to check writing assignments. Another type of software that might be useful in teaching foreign languages are online translation dictionaries. These programs allow you to type in a word or phrase in one language and immediately display the equivalent expression in another language. They are quicker to use than printed dictionaries and could save money if you wanted to provide one to every student (i.e., by means of a networked system). One new development is this area is the use of CD-ROM to store online dictionaries. For example, the Languages of the World CD-ROM disk from NTC Publishing Group contains eighteen bilingual dictionaries covering twelve languages (more than seven million words)!

Computers That Talk

Hearing the correct pronunciation of words and phrases is a critical aspect of learning a new language. For computers to be truly useful in language learning, they must be able to produce spoken output. There are a number of ways this can be done.

The best quality sound is typically produced when the speech is recorded and stored in analog format on a videodisc or CD-ROM. This is the same process as recording audio for audio or videotapes, except that sequences on videodisc and CD-ROM can be accessed randomly by the computer. This means that a given word or sentence can be found and played back instantly even though there may be thousands of such sequences on the disc. The only drawback to this approach is that you need a videodisc or CD-ROM player to hear the sound.

It is possible to store sound on the same magnetic storage media (floppy or hard disks) used to store computer information. To do this, we must digitize the sound, i.e., convert it into digital format. Many companies make interface cards or devices for personal computers that accomplish this task. You simply talk into a microphone attached to your computer and everything you say is stored in digital form. Each sound can be called up by a program when you want to use it. However, there is a major limitation to this form of storing sound—it takes up a tremendous amount of disk space. For example, a single word might require 10K bytes. So a vocabulary of 100 words would require 1,000K (1 megabyte).

The third way to produce sound is not to store it at all but to synthesize it as needed. Words and phrases are presented by phonetic representations that correspond to sounds that the computer can make. The advantage of this approach is that the computer can make sounds that were not prerecorded (e.g., student names, sentences typed in). The major disadvantage is that synthesized speech is usually difficult to understand—computers are not blessed with the wonderful sound generation capability of the human vocal system.

HyperGlot

HyperGlot Software Company in Knoxville, Tennessee, specializes in programs for foreign language learning. Here are some examples of the kinds of programs they provide (see Figure 9-1):

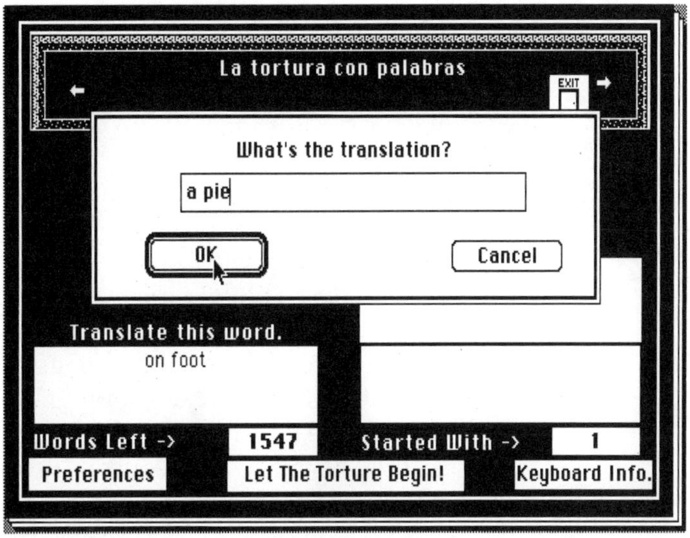

Figure 9-1 An example of a foreign language learning program (Hyperglot Software Co.)

- Word Torture—Drill on 1400-1600 of the most commonly used verbs, nouns, adjectives, adverbs, and comparatives (Russian, Spanish, French, German, Italian).

- Pronunciation Tutors—Use digitized sound to help students learn the correct pronunciation and intonation of words (Spanish, French, German, Chinese, Japanese).

- Verb Tutors—Extensive drills in verb conjugation and the proper use of all tenses based on 200 sentences (Russian, Spanish, French, German, Italian).

- Grammar Exercises—complete course on grammar including interactive exercises (Spanish, French).

One of the important features of many of these programs is that they can be modified by the teacher or student, including addition or replacing words. This means that the programs can be customized to fit particular lessons or learning assignments (see Figure 9-2).

In addition to selling these programs individually, Hyperglot also markets them all on a single CD-ROM called *LinguaROM*.

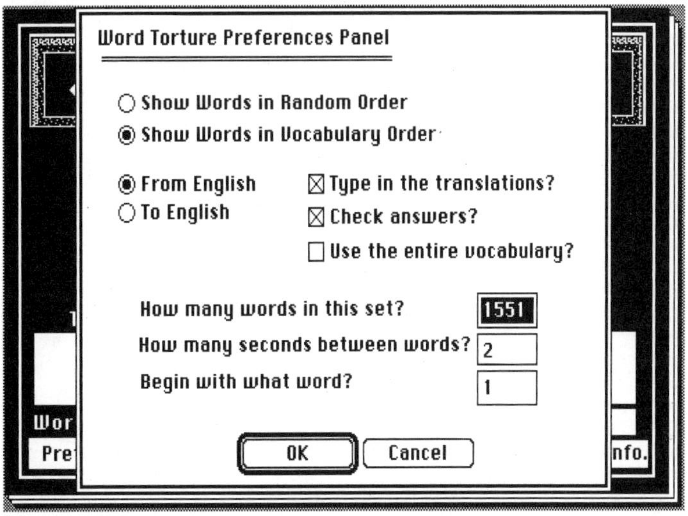

Figure 9-2 Language Learning programs can be modified to suit individual requirements (Hyperglot Software Co.)

Interactive Videodisc and CD-ROM

A great deal of work has been done with interactive videodisc for foreign language learning. Interactive videodisc is ideal for language learning because it allows photographs and video sequences to be included in the instruction as well as recorded audio. For example, a videodisc program for learning Spanish called El Avion Hispano (developed at Cornell University) places the student in the role of a writer on an airplane flight. The assignment is to learn as much as possible about the other passengers on the flight, which can be accomplished by viewing still photographs, video sequences, and text information.

Another interesting example is the Salamandre videodisc that illustrates the architecture of fifteenth- and sixteenth-century chateaux in France's Loire Valley. The videodisc includes narrated "fly-bys" and "walk-throughs" of the castles in both English and French. Animation shows the evolution of the chateaux from feudal strongholds to luxury dwellings. Materials such as this can be used to teach language in the context of history and culture.

At the U.S. Naval Academy in Annapolis, Maryland, interactive videodisc is used extensively in teaching foreign languages. However, the emphasis at the Naval Academy is on the use of videodisc to provide "authentic" foreign language experiences. Television broadcasts from other countries are received via satellite, recorded on videotape, and then mastered onto videodiscs. Instructors select the portions of broadcasts that they wish to use and programs are written to access these sequences. The value of this approach is that students are exposed to foreign languages as they are actually spoken and used in real contexts.

Recently, software developers have started to take advantage of the multimedia storage capacity of CD-ROM for language learning applications. For example, the Voyager Company markets a CD-ROM for the Macintosh called *Exotic Japan* that provides over 1600 sounds of traditional Japanese music and native speech in both male and female voices. The disc offers three different modes of navigation: lesson, quiz, or game.

The names and addresses of companies that market videodisc and CD-ROM products are provided at the end of this chapter.

Developing Your Own Programs

Although most teachers find that commercially available programs and materials meet their needs, some teachers develop their own. Edwina Spodark, a French teacher at Hollins College in Roanoke, Virginia, explains why:

Although I have written over a hundred programs for use in my beginning and intermediate French classes, a semester never goes by when I don't have to write at least two or three more at students' request. I write drill and practice programs on various aspects of French grammar for my students to do as homework on our VAX 11/780. So far this semester, it's been programs for the conjugation of the irregular verbs vivre, suivre, and voir as well as a more complicated series on the past participle agreement rules. These programs eliminate the endless paper grading for me and provide the students with opportunity to practice what they need to in order to master the material. They also receive immediate correction and feedback so they know right away if they are having trouble.

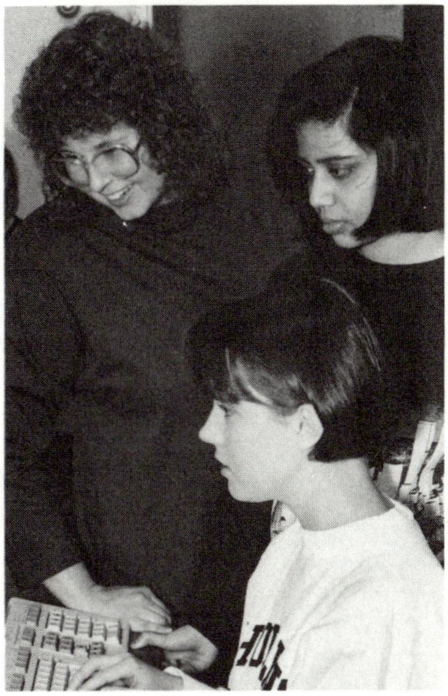

Edwina describes the value of using the computer in her foreign language teaching:

My students learned firsthand the value of these programs. As a general rule, after I made the computer programs mandatory, test grades actually went up for some students and test averages on the whole remained relatively high. It also became obvious that students who usually required more time to master certain material were no longer being left behind. I am able to devote larger amounts of class time to other areas of language instruction such as conversation and pronunciation that, in the past, have been pushed into the background because of the need to cover difficult grammar structures. I also find that the explanatory prefaces that I write for each drill sequence serve as a permanent reference source for students and thus provide them with help when I am unavailable.

The benefits of using computers described by Edwina Spodark would be achieved whether she developed her own programs or not. But by writing programs herself, she is able to create materials that fill an immediate need in her classroom. The book by Vockell (1987) provides examples of BASIC programs for language arts. (See chapter 10 for more about developing your own software.)

Summary

Computers can help language learning in a number of ways:

- Providing drills that allow students to practice basic vocabulary and grammar as much as they need to.

- Providing multimedia learning experiences that present language in realistic settings.

- Allowing students of many countries to interact directly via electronic mail and computer conferences.

- Providing speech output so that students can hear the pronunciation of languages.

- Providing online dictionaries and other translation software that can make language learning easier.

As the world becomes more multicultural, language learning is sure to become an increasingly important subject in schools. Computers may help us teach it better.

Further Information

If you want to find out more about the application of computers to language learning, the best source is the *C.A.L.L.* (Computer Assisted Language Learning) *Journal* published by CALICO. You might also want to examine the books by Smith (1987) or Vockell (1987).

CALICO, 3078 JKHB, Brigham Young University, Provo, UT 84602. (801) 378-7079. An international consortium dedicated to the application of technology to the teaching of languages.

Smith, W. F. (1987). *Modern Media in Foreign Language Education: Theory and Implementation.* Lincolnwood, IL: National Textbook Co.

Vockell, E. (1987). *Model Programs for Instruction.* Englewood Cliffs, NJ: Prentice-Hall.

The following companies market videodiscs or CD-ROMs for educational applications and offer free catalogs:

Bureau of Electronic Publishing, 141 New Rd., Parsippany, NJ 07054. (800) 828-4766.

EduCorp, 531 Stevens Ave, Suite B, Solana Beach, CA 92075. (800) 843-9497.

Optical Data Corporation, 30 Technology Dr., Warren, NJ 07060. (201) 668-0022.

VideoDiscovery, 1515 Dexter Ave. N., #400, Seattle, WA 98109. (206) 285-5400.

The Voyager Company. 1351 Pacific Coast Highway, Santa Monica, CA 90401. (800) 446-2001.

Warner New Media, 3500 W. Olive Blvd., Suite 1050, Burbank, CA 91505. (818) 955-9999.

Activities

• Obtain at least two foreign language drill programs in the language you teach. Try them out from the point of view of your students. How could you use them in your teaching? Would they be worthwhile?

• If you have a videodisc player available, obtain a videodisc designed for the language you teach and familiarize yourself with the content. Would this disk be more useful if used by yourself with the whole class, by students in small discussion groups, or by students individually?

• Develop a lesson plan for a network project that allows students from different countries to interact and learn each other's language and culture. Try to think of something that will get students highly involved and motivated to interact.

• Develop a lesson plan for a cross-disciplinary activity that involves the use of computers for language learning and one or more other subjects (e.g., math, art, history).

• Obtain an authoring system and try making up a program to teach some aspect of grammar that students always have trouble with. You might want to try a number of different instructional strategies to discover which one works best.

Chapter 10 Understanding Computers

So far in this book we have examined the many ways that teachers can use computers to be more effective and productive. In general we have ignored any technical discussion about computers themselves. It should be clear that you can use computers to teach quite well without knowing very much about the details of how they work.

However, computers are a worthy subject of study in their own right. They are an important element of most organizations and many people use them to do their jobs. As consumers, we constantly encounter them when we go shopping, travel, or do our banking. For children, computer-based games are a common form of play. The use of computers also raises important ethical and philosophical issues having to do with privacy and access to information.

Programming has become a major subject area at all colleges and most high schools. Not only is learning programming important for students who pursue a computer-related vocation, but it is also essential background for anyone preparing to be a scientist or engineer. And, for teachers who want to develop their own computer-based curriculum materials, some knowledge of software design principles is highly desirable.

In this chapter we discuss the topic of computer literacy, the teaching of programming, and the subject of authoring computer-based materials.

Computer Literacy

The subject of computer literacy has been an educational "hot potato" for a long time. The fundamental issue is whether computers should be taught as a separate subject or whether they should be integrated into the rest of the curriculum. The answer seems to be both.

Many schools offer a survey course about computers that covers the nature of hardware and software, applications, issues, and computers' impact on society. The goal of such courses is to create an informed citizen who can understand the strengths and limitations of technology. A second level of computer literacy is a "hands-on" course in which students are required to learn basic applications programs such as word processing, spreadsheets, databases, graphics, and telecommunications. This kind of course is provided at many universities as a prerequisite for taking other courses that involve the use of computers. It is also given to many teachers and school staff as inservice training.

As far as integrating computers into the curriculum is concerned, most of this book has focused on that theme. Obviously, this is a much more demanding level of computer literacy for you and your students than when it is taught as self-contained subject matter. To understand computers at a level where you can modify what and how you teach, you must know what computers can do. In most cases, this means becoming familiar with specific software packages or application programs.

Preparing the Managers of Tomorrow

One of the most practical applications of computer literacy is in business education classes. A business education curriculum developed by the Eden Prairie Public Schools in Eden Prairie, Minnesota, illustrates how computer literacy can be integrated into school activities and meet the needs of local employers. The curriculum covers three areas: nature of the business enterprise, information management, and business communications. The rationale for the program is explained by Karl Beach, director of technology:

> *The community wanted more problem solving in our business courses. After high school our students go on to further study and eventually into management positions. So the community asked us to develop the student's higher-order thinking skills and to focus on the managerial aspects of business—rather than on keystrokes and secretarial training.*

Karl explains the significance of spreadsheets, graphics, and databases in this curriculum:

To a manager, the whole picture is important. Spreadsheets are important because they have cells that allow you to quantify things, but they also allow you to represent the data graphically. So a spreadsheet is a viewing device—a tool that lets you see the general from the particular. You also have to decide which aspect of your message is most important and which medium will best get it across. Creating a database is a form of problem solving. You need a clear idea of what you're trying to keep track of before you build it.

Understanding computers is clearly an essential element in this attempt to prepare the managers of tomorrow.

Programming

Teaching programming can take place at three different levels. At the college level, computer science courses involve fundamental concepts such as algorithms, data structures, compiler design, numerical analysis, operating systems, software engineering, artificial intelligence, user interface design, and so on. At the middle and secondary school level, programming classes tend to focus on learning a specific language such as Pascal or BASIC and writing programs using that language. At the elementary and preschool level, most programming activities involve LOGO and the focus is on learning basic concepts in other subjects using LOGO as a tool. (See also the discussion of computational science in Chapter 6)

Marian Rosen is a teacher for the Ladue Schools in St. Louis, Missouri. She has been working with LOGO for many years. Here is how she describes the significance of LOGO:

I teach LOGO the way I used to teach art. I introduce an idea and then challenge students to use it in their own way to compete a project that is unique but which fulfills some teacher-made parameters.

Most of the time, children in school are starved for "real" experiences. Kids have some sense that a lot of the experiences they have in school aren't real but are just watered-down "school" exercises. One of the wonderful things about LOGO is the way it brings school and the world together, helping to demystify certain everyday things students see around them.

The plastic building blocks called LEGO and the programming language called LOGO have more in common than their names. Both are based on the powerful idea that you can take a handful of simple forms (in LEGO the blocks and in LOGO the primitives) and combine them to build ever larger and more complex forms. Both are so carefully crafted that they are reliable paths to learning in the real world. Both allow students of all ages to become involved in projects that are meaningful to them and that encourage different learning styles. Both are fun. Both present a challenge to educators—they are so versatile and so rich in promise that we must find time for them in schools.

We should be wary of getting embroiled in a "which computer language is best" argument. Somebody once observed that programming is not a science or craft—but a religion, with specific computer languages being the gospel. The "best" computer language is the one that you happen to know, that you have available, and that will do the job. Furthermore, computer languages come and go, so you have to be prepared to learn a new one every few years to stay current.

One of the important aspects of any programming language selected for use in schools is the quality and extent of the debugging utilities and source code libraries available. Debugging utilities allow programmers to discover program "bugs" easily. Source code libraries are collections of sample programs that can be reused to create new programs. The Turbo series of programming languages (Turbo Pascal, Turbo Prolog, Turbo C, Turbo BASIC and others) from Borland International come with extensive debugging tools and source code libraries and are popular at schools and colleges. TrueBASIC is another company that provides an extensive library of programs that demonstrate and extend BASIC programming.

LOGO: Learning by Doing

LOGO is a programming language specifically designed for children. It was originally developed by Seymour Papert at MIT and is now used by schools all over the world. LOGO is intended as a tool that children can use to explore concepts and solve problems. It applies just as much to art or music instruction as it does to math or science learning.

A key metaphor associated with LOGO is the "turtle." In an attempt to make LOGO activities concrete for young children, a robot that resembled a turtle was developed. The movement and behavior of the turtle was controlled by LOGO programs. Later versions of LOGO present a computer-animated turtle on the computer screen instead of using an actual robot device.

LOGO is both simple to learn and very powerful. Here is a sample LOGO program that draws a circular line for the specified number of degrees:

```
TO CIRCLE : DEGREES
IF: DEGREES = 0 STOP
FORWARD 1
ROTATE LEFT 1
CIRCLE : DEGREES -1
END
```

Even though the LOGO language has a syntax and semantics simple enough for children to learn easily, it includes many advanced programming features. For example, the CIRCLE program above uses recursion (in the second to last line) in which the program repeats itself until the stopping criterion in the first line is met. Because LOGO has such advanced features, it allows children to express and explore powerful ideas.

LogoWriter extends the LOGO language in a number of ways. It provides a text editor that makes it easy to write LOGO programs as well as reports. LogoWriter allows up to four different turtles on the screen that can be active simultaneously. LogoWriter also provides a number of additional commands that make it easier to create graphics. These extra features of LogoWriter make it suitable for writing interactive documents.

LEGO LOGO is the combination of LEGO building blocks and the LOGO programing language. LEGO LOGO involves a special interface to Apple II computers and blocks that contain motors, sensors, lights, gears, and counters. Students can build vehicles, machines, robots and almost any kind of device they can imagine.

The original MIT version of LOGO is distributed by Terrapin, (207) 878-8200. LogoWriter is marketed by LCSI, (800) 321-LOGO. LEGO LOGO is available from LEGO Systems, (203) 749-2291.

Authoring

Some day in a moment of sheer madness you may decide that you want to develop your own program. It might be some form of learning activity for your students (e.g., a drill, game, or simulation) or it might be a utility for yourself. Almost every teacher who has done this would give you a standard piece of advice: don't try developing your own software until you are sure that you can't buy it somewhere!

Why? Developing software is a tedious and time-consuming business. It takes a long time to completely debug and test a program. It also takes a lot of effort to come up with a design that does what you want. Something that makes sense to you may not make sense to other people when they use your program. The development of commercial software often takes many months (sometimes years) and involves a team of experienced software designers and programmers. Creating a computer program is like making a movie. There are lots of steps involved and you need lots of expertise. Of course, if we are talking home movies instead of Hollywood, it's not such a big undertaking.

The amount of effort required to actually implement a program depends on what kind of programming language or authoring software you use. For instructional applications, there are many authoring languages and systems available. Authoring languages are specialized programming languages designed specifically for creating instructional programs. Some popular ones are Tencore and PILOT. Authoring systems allow you to create programs without any programming and are ideal for teachers with no programming background.

Without any doubt, HyperCard for the Apple Macintosh is the most popular authoring tool used today in schools. HyperCard makes it easy to create a program without having to worry much about programming details. The Cincinnati Country Day School in Cincinnati, Ohio illustrates how HyperCard can be used across all grade levels. Here are some of the ways HyperCard is used at the school:

- In English class, students studying American literature create stacks to describe the characteristics of romanticism, realism, and modernism. They use art from videodiscs and digitize music from the various periods to include in their stacks.
- In a fifth grade math class, students use the junk mail received at their homes to learn about percentages and statistics. They use HyperCard to organize, retrieve, and evaluate the data.
- In a third grade class studying Egyptian tombs, each student receives a "tomb" stack to personalize. They can make drawings on the walls and build objects that might have been left in the tomb by the king's family.
- HyperCard stacks are used in science classrooms as an alternative to lab experiments that can be costly, dangerous, and difficult to control. Students create stacks that allow them to quickly and safely see the results of their experiments.

Joe Hofmeister, computer coordinator at the school has these comments about the use of HyperCard:

> *Classrooms need to become more centered on learning instead of teaching. Students are creating their own knowledge. We need to let the kids see what they can do. One of the things that is so remarkable about HyperCard is that the tools become transparent for the students. They focus on the issues and content rather than the technology. Students and teachers are walking a new pathway of*

information. None of us is comfortable with the machinery—cords, cables, and drivers. For people not steeped in computer science, it's a jungle. But the rewards are great for those courageous enough to jump in and try.

What Is HyperCard?

HyperCard is an authoring system developed and marketed by Apple for the Macintosh computer. Because it comes with the computer, almost everyone who owns a Macintosh now has HyperCard. This means that if you develop a HyperCard program (called a "stack"), you can be sure that it will run on lots of machines without the need to buy any additional software.

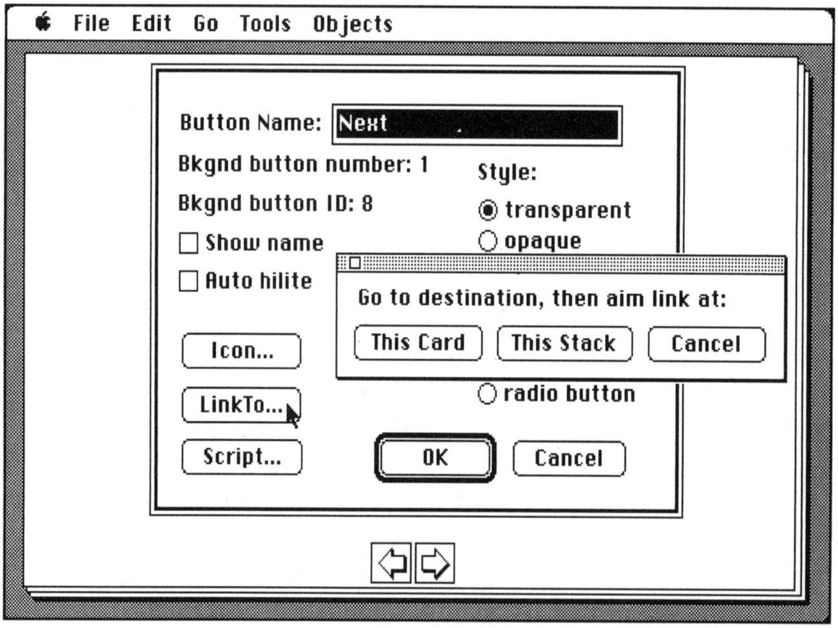

Figure 10-1 Sample HyperCard stack card (Apple Computer Inc.)

A HyperCard stack consists of one or more "cards" that usually correspond to separate screens. A card can contain text fields, graphics, or buttons. Buttons are used to specify branching links from one card to another. To create a link between one card and another, you simply define a button (which can have almost any format desired) and then identify which card you want linked to that button (see Figure 10-1). HyperCard provides a simple set of graphics tools to create screens or you can use any other graphics program.

One powerful aspect of HyperCard is that it is based on an English-like programming language called HyperTalk. HyperTalk lets you write procedures to control how cards, fields, and buttons behave. For example, the sequence of HyperTalk commands below produces a screen showing a map of Africa, plays some music, and then displays a dialog box with three options:

```
on mouseUp
   visual effect dissolve
   go to card "Africa"
   play "jungle"
   answer "Are you ready for an an adventure?" with
      "Ok" or "Help" or "Cancel"
   if it is "Ok" then
      go to card "Start"
   else if it is "Help"
      go to card "Help"
   end if
end mouseUp
```

HyperCard has resulted in a virtual explosion of programs for classroom use largely developed by teachers and students. Stacks are often available from their developers at no charge or for nominal cost. There are also companies that specialize in distributing stacks such as Heizer Software and EduCorp. (See discussion of the Educator HomeCard in Chapter 2.)

Programs similar to HyperCard for other computers include Linkway (IBM), HyperPad (Brightbill-Roberts), and Toolbox (Asymetrix) for the IBM PC and compatibles; HyperStudio (Roger Wagner Publishing) and TutorTech (Techware) for Apple IIs; and AmigaVision (Commodore) for the Amiga. A number of other programs for the Macintosh such as SuperCard (Silicon Beach) and Plus (Olduvai) have additional capabilities. The point is that HyperCard (and its clones) represents a new generation of authoring software that makes it much easier to develop programs.

Summary

Computer literacy refers to knowing how computers can be used and the implications of these applications. Programming means knowing a programming language and being able to write programs. Authoring describes the process of developing software and creating your own programs. As a teacher you may be interested in some, all or none of these perspectives.

Many teachers have found LOGO (and extensions such as LogoWriter or LEGO LOGO) useful in the classroom, especially with young children. It provides a "thinking tool" that students can use to explore concepts, solve problems, or be creative. It works in subjects as diverse as art, music, language arts, mathematics, and science. It is also an excellent way to introduce students to programming and computers.

Many teachers are discovering that authoring tools such as HyperCard allow them (or their students) to create programs that make teaching or learning more interesting and fun. However, regardless of which programming or authoring tool you use, you still have to know something about how to design good software. Luckily there are many books that explain the do's and don'ts of software design (see Further Information).

Further Information

If you are interested in the topic of computer literacy, you might want to examine one of the many computer literacy textbooks available such as Mandell (1987), Sullivan, Lewis, & Cook (1988), Sanders (1983), or Wessells (1990).

If you want to learn more about HyperCard and HyperTalk, see Apple (1988), Goodman (1990), or Waite (1989). Some good references for LOGO are Friendly (1988), Harper (1989), Papert (1980), Thornburg (1986), Watt & Watt (1987) or Weir (1986). The ISTE also publishes a number of books about LOGO.

To learn more about the authoring process and the use of design software, see Allessi & Trollip (1990), Hannafin & Peck (1988), Kearsley (1986), Laurel (1990), or Price (1991). The book by Mayer (1988) discusses current research on teaching and learning how to program.

References

Allessi, S. & Trollip, S. (1990). *Computer-Based Instruction: Methods and Development (2nd edition).* Englewood Cliffs, NJ: Prentice-Hall.

Apple Inc. (1988). *HyperCard Stack Design Guidelines.* Reading, MA: Addison-Wesley.

Friendly, M. (1988). *Advanced LOGO.* Hillsdale, NJ: Erlbaum Associates. (Accompanying software for Apple II and IBM PC.)

Goodman, D. (1990). *The Complete HyperCard Handbook (revised edition).* New York: Bantam.

Hannafin, M. J., & Peck, K. (1988). *The Design, Development and Evaluation of Instructional Software.* New York: Macmillan Publishing Co.

Harper, D. (1989). *LOGO: Theory and Practice.* Belmont, CA: Brooks/Cole.

Kearsley, G. (1986). *Authoring: The Design of Instructional Software.* Reading, MA: Addison-Wesley.

Laurel, B. (1990). *The Art of Interface Design.* Reading, MA: Addison-Wesley.

Mandell, S. (1987). *Computers and Information Processing (4th edition).* St. Paul, MN: West Publishing Co.

Mayer, R. E. (1988). *Teaching and Learning Computer Programming.* Hillsdale, NJ: Erlbaum Associates.

Papert. S. (1980). *Mindstorms: Children, Computers, and Powerful Ideas.* New York: Basic Books.

Price, R. (1991). *Computer-Aided Instruction: A Guide for Authors.* Belmont, CA: Wadsworth.

Sanders, D. H. (1983). *Computers Today.* New York: McGraw-Hill.

Sullivan, D. R., Lewis, T. G. & Cook, C. R. (1988). *Computing Today.* Boston: Houghton Mifflin.

Thornburg, D. (1986). *Beyond Turtle Graphics.* Reading, MA: Addison-Wesley.

Waite Group (1989). *Tricks of the HyperTalk Masters.* Indianapolis, IN: Hayden Books.

Watt, M., & Watt, D. (1987). *Teaching with LOGO: Building Blocks for Learning.* Reading, MA: Addison-Wesley.

Weir, S. (1986). *Cultivating Minds: A LOGO Case Book.* New York: Harper & Row.

Wessells, M. (1990). *Computer, Self and Society.* Englewood Cliffs, NJ: Prentice-Hall.

Activities

Here are some activities for learning more about computers:

- Obtain a computer literacy textbook and skim through it. Do you see anything that has implications for your own teaching?

- If you have never used HyperCard, find someone who has and have him or her give you a short demonstration. Does watching the demonstration give you any ideas about "stacks" that you might want to create?

- Find a teacher or student who is familiar with LOGO and ask him or her to show you how to write LOGO programs. How could you use LOGO in your own teaching?

- Investigate a number of authoring programs for a particular computer. How do their features and capabilities compare? Which one appeals to you most? Why?

- Interview someone who has developed his or her own software. What was the most difficult aspect? What lessons were learned? What advice would he or she give?

Chapter 11
Creativity and The Arts

Historically, computer use in education has focused on math and language learning. However, computers are wonderful tools for artists too. During the past decade, many art and music teachers discovered that they could unleash the creativity of their students using computers. Computer art and music activities give students a chance to learn by doing rather than by passive appreciation or mindless mimicry. More recently, it has become possible to create video productions using personal computers, allowing students to get involved in creating television productions that bring together pictures, sound, and motion.

Computer as Canvas

The capability to draw on a computer screen with a paint or draw program fascinates most kids (and many adults). A wide variety of paint and draw programs are available for all personal computers, ranging from very simple to extremely sophisticated. Art activities that involve the use of such software are popular at all grade levels.

In elementary classrooms, computers allow young children to develop their creative power and enhance their visual thinking ability. A common use of graphics programs is to have students draw or illustrate stories. LOGO (see chapter 10) can also be used to let students create simple drawings (such as flowers or animals) by writing simple programs. At the secondary and college level, students frequently use graphics programs to create designs or make sketches. In many vocational programs, using the computer to create graphic art is an important career skill.

Painting versus Drawing Software

To create graphics on a computer screen, you need to use a painting or drawing program. Although both types of software look similar, there is an important difference between the two. Both have menus of painting/drawing "tools" down the side (icons represent lines, circles, rectangles, etc.) as well as palettes of colors or patterns along the top or bottom rows. However, when you create something on the screen with a paint program, the elements of your graphic are independent and can only be manipulated as areas of the screen. When you create something on the screen with a drawing program, each element of your graphic can be manipulated as a separate object. This is why drawing programs are often called "object-oriented" graphics as opposed to the "bit-mapped" graphics of paint programs.

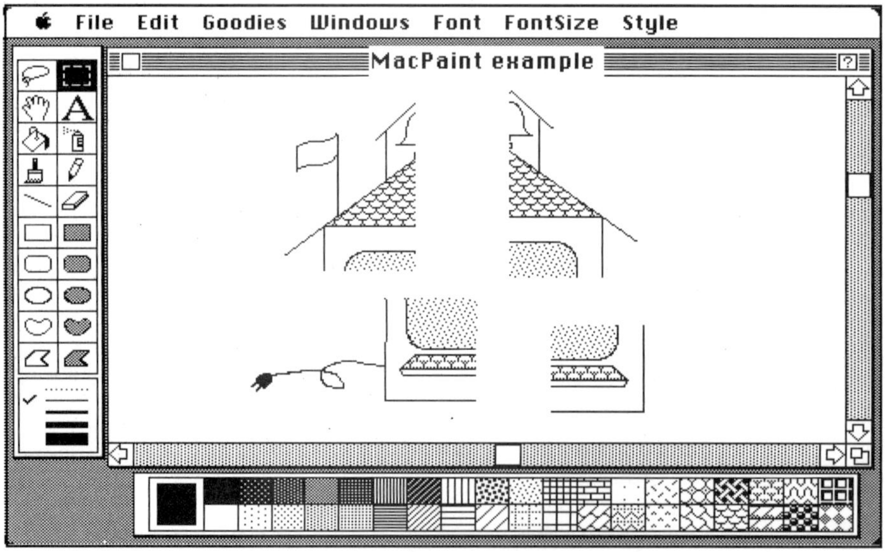

Figure 11-1 MacPaint example (Apple Computer Inc.).

The screens in Figures 11-1 and 11-2 illustrate this point using the *MacPaint* and *MacDraw* programs.

In the MacPaint example in Figure 11-1, the image can only be worked with in sections. In this case it has been divided into four pieces. In the MacDraw example in Figure 11-2, the individual components of the image are separate objects and can be manipulated separately.

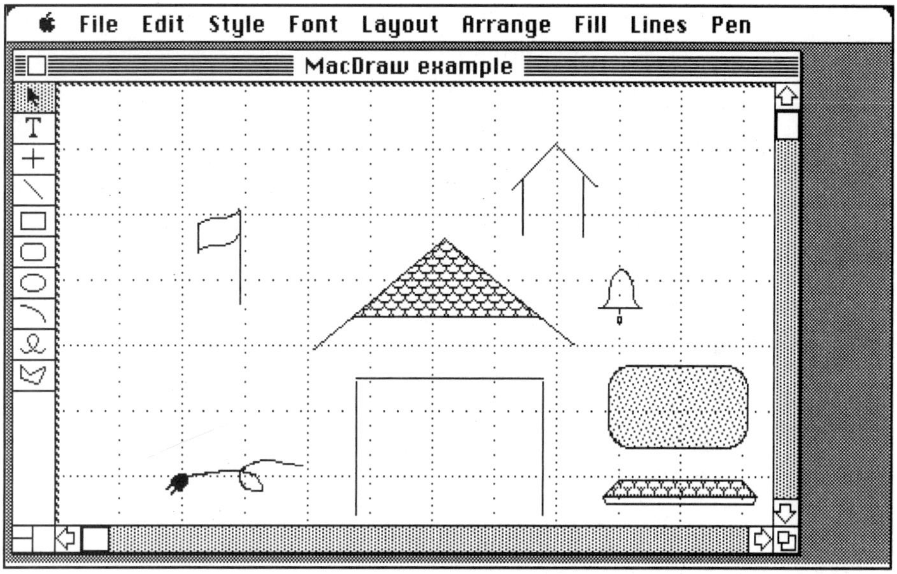

Figure 11-2 MacDraw example (Apple Computer Inc.).

Some graphics programs provide both painting and drawing capabilities.

In advanced art classes students use graphics programs to experiment with different styles of art. For example, they can try to reproduce abstract or expressionist paintings in order to understand the factors that underlie their composition. Graphics software makes it easy to change colors, shading, and position. Photographs or prints of paintings can be scanned using a digitizer to provide material for students to work with. If a videodisc or CR-ROM player is available, reproductions can be loaded from a disc and displayed directly on the screen.

Joan Kay is an art teacher at Poughkeepsie Day School in Poughkeepsie, New York. She has found a number of ways to use the computer to make other subjects come alive, especially history. For example, she gave a middle school class studying the Renaissance the assignment of designing their own stained-glass window patterns, based on the historical examples in books. Joan feels that because the computer screen is illuminated from the back, it produces lighting effects similar to actual stained glass windows.

Another computer activity she has explored with students is the design of quilt patterns as they relate to American history. She thinks the computer is ideal for quilt design because students can easily try out different combinations of colors and patterns. However, because she views computers as a design tool, she still has her students create actual stained-glass pieces or quilts after they are satisfied with their design.

Videodisc Art Collections

One of the problems in art education has always been access to great works of art. Videodisc provides a wonderful way to overcome this problem as well as a way to provide students with interesting art history projects. The National Gallery of Art and the Louvre have put a large portion of their collections on videodiscs. In addition, videodiscs on Vincent Van Gogh, Picasso, and Andrew Wyeth are available. These discs can be used for class demonstrations or by students for individual projects. Using an authoring program such as HyperCard, students can assemble works in any order they wish, adding their own comments or narration. This makes it possible for students to become personally involved in art studies.

Figure 11-3 Visual Almanac Menu (Apple Computer Inc.).

One product worthy of special mention in this regard is the Visual Almanac developed by Apple Multimedia Laboratory and marketed by Intellimation. The Visual Almanac consists of a videodisc, CD-ROM, and print guide. It contains over 7,000 different images including movies, animations and still photographs, as well as 150 sounds (a total of 22 megabytes of information). The images and sounds are organized into collections such as solar systems, studies in time, American history, animals, and so on (see Figure 11-3). The Almanac also includes a series of 14 activities and a composition workspace that can be used to assemble new works. The intent of the Almanac is to provide teachers and students with a multimedia database that can be used for any curriculum area or creative pursuit.

Can Anyone Be a Computer Artist?

One of the interesting questions that computer art raises is the nature of artistic talent and creativity. With the kinds of sophisticated functions provided by many paint and drawing programs, does natural talent matter as much? David Kreisberg, a computer resource teacher at the Pullen Arts Magnet School in Maryland, describes his experiences:

The computer doesn't make anyone an artist any more than a desktop publishing program makes someone a good layout designer. When I taught painting programs to students, I tried to stay out of the art education aspect and focused on the computer as a tool for making art. We did spend time analyzing paintings from art galleries and using some activities from art books but that was secondary to exploiting the unique capabilities of the computer as an artistic medium. We also analyzed computer paintings to learn about techniques. What knowledge of drawing I have came in handy in terms of helping students do problem solving—for example, what was the best way to create a gradient of colors to be used for shading?

On the importance of the use of computers in the arts, he comments:

The use of computers for art is not perceived as a meaningful activity in most schools. I think that the general perception is that computers should be used for writing, math, and support of the "serious" academic subjects. Art and music classes do not have the same kind of access to computers, even though they are used in "the real world" for both of these fields.

Animation

Computers can be used to extend traditional forms of art, and they can also make a unique contribution in the area of animation. Using animation software such as the Animation Studio (Disney Software) or Director (MacroMind), students and teachers can create cartoons or simple movies. For example, Richard Starr teamed up with math teacher Margot Maddock at the Francis Richmond School in Hanover, New Hampshire to create an animation called "Slope" to teach the concept of rise versus run. The animation focuses on a bicycle rider who rides up an inclined plane and a dog who climbs stairs to illustrate the principles involved. This work was done using a Commodore Amiga, a relatively inexpensive computer that is especially suited to art and animation activities. (See additional discussion of animation for mathematics in Chapter 7.)

The Amiga is also used in the art classes at T. C. Williams High School in Alexandria, Virginia. Using the computer and videotape equipment, the students complete projects in art theory and technique. First they prepare storyboards and scripts for their projects, use the computer to generate the artwork, and then record their productions on videocassette, sometimes introducing external images and live action. In addition to learning about art, the projects provide problem-solving and peer teaching opportunities. Furthermore, students often carry their computer graphics and animation skills into other curriculum areas. They can employ the same technology used for artistic expression as tools for visual presentations in science and social studies.

A Potpourri of Programs for the Arts

Many fascinating programs have been developed by teachers for various aspects of the arts. Here is a brief list of such software for the Macintosh:

- Escher-Sketch—Lets artists sketch motifs and then manipulate the motifs to create a wallpaper-type pattern. (Can also be used in mathematics to explore plane symmetry groups.)

- MacPhotography Workshop—A simulation program that teaches novices how to use a 35mm camera and darkroom equipment. Covers use of camera, developing film, making contact sheets and enlargements.

- The TheaterGame—A simulation that lets you stage and direct a play. Provides a library of stages, props, and characters. You create an animated movie of scenes complete with moving characters.

- Origami—An introduction to the Japanese art of paper folding, including animated instructions for making popular constructions.

- Hometown—A clip-art collection that provides the layouts for fifteen miniature buildings along with a selection of doors, windows, and other architectural structures. Designs can be printed and assembled.

Most of these programs are available from Intellimation.

Electronic Music

One of the remarkable areas of computer development has been in the electronic music world. As soon as computers appeared, musicians began to explore their potential to create new forms of music, particularly through the use of electronic synthesizers. With the appearance of personal computers, many amateur musicians got into the act and the range and use of computers in music increased dramatically. Today, personal computers can be used to compose, edit, and print musical scores as well as to control the play and recording of electronic instruments. Much of this is made possible by a special computer language called MIDI (Musical Instrument Digital Interface) that allows musical sequences to be stored and processed by computers. These developments in electronic music have changed not only the music industry but also the fundamental nature of music education.

Computers can play a variety of different roles in schools. One common use is to provide students with a good selection of instruments via synthesizers. For example, at Marrs Junior High School in Omaha, Nebraska, music teacher Jeff Ingraham relies on his computer to play the instruments that would otherwise be missing in a school concert. He feels that it helps fill out the sound of the student orchestra and produces a more professional concert. Of course, the machine is also used by students to compose and print musical scores. Ingraham has been creating a tutorial program to teach students about musical notation.

In fact, the use of drill and tutorial programs to teach music theory and fundamentals is another important application of computers in schools. Such programs range from simple games designed to teach notation or chording to more advanced tutorials on particular techniques or theory. In most cases the programs either generate sounds or can be connected to instruments through a MIDI link, so the learning is "hands-on."

Multimedia Music Appreciation

Compact discs (CDs) have quickly surpassed cassettes as the medium for audio recordings, and CD-ROM is fast becoming a popular way for distributing multimedia databases. Two interesting CD-ROM products are the Beethoven Symphony No. 9 program from Voyager and the Magic Flute Audio Notes program from Warner New Media. Both programs involve CDs and HyperCard stacks to be used with Apple Macintosh computers.

The Beethoven program was developed by UCLA professor of music Robert Winter and includes text, graphics, and audio sequences intended to enhance the listener's experience of Symphony No. 9. (see Figure 11-4) It is possible to request a commentary on the music as it is being played, examine the historical setting in which the music was written, or look up terms in a glossary, including actual examples from the symphony.

The Magic Flute program provides the opera and music on three CD-ROMs. While the opera is progressing, you can switch between the German

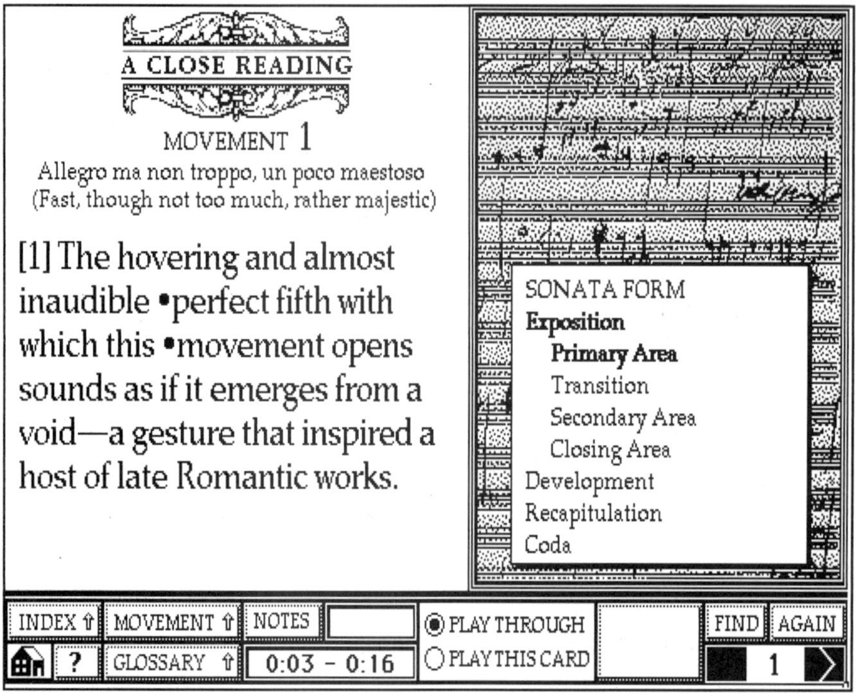

Figure 11-4 The Beethoven Symphony No. 9 Stack (Voyager Co.)

libretto, an English translation, a synopsis of the story, and a musical analysis. There is also a glossary with examples from the opera and a number of other features. One especially interesting aspect of the Magic Flute program is that the music is stored in MIDI format and can be accessed by MIDI software.

Both of these programs are the first in a series to be marketed by the two companies. They illustrate the kind of impressive new materials available to music educators—provided you have the right equipment (in this case, a CD-ROM player and a Macintosh)!

Video Arts

Video has become an important creative medium in the Information Age. Many teachers have their students create videotapes for class projects. Computers can be useful in such projects for writing scripts, producing graphics and animations, or creating musical scores. Terri Nighswonger, a history teacher in Livermore, California describes a video project conducted by her eighth grade class:

> *This year each team of students created a graphic picture of their vision of America and these were then recorded on videocassette with music. This production was then sent to the Soviet Union as a follow-up of a visit we experienced from the Soviets earlier in the year. We also used the VCR Companion program to make an introduction and conclusion for this production.*

The students of the Hill Vocational Center in Lansing, Michigan produce a weekly newscast that is broadcast live over a local cable channel. Computers are used to produce the special effects used in the newscast including overlay titles, the program logo, and illustrations for stories. The newscast reinforces the skills taught in many classes and gives a "real-world" focus to the curriculum.

Fifth grade students at College Oaks Elementary School in Lake Charles, Louisiana also produce a newscast for a local cable channel as a joint language arts and social studies project. Students use word processing to write and edit their scripts for stories, interviews, commercials, and weather reports. They then go out into the community to tape their material. Back at school, they use the computer to edit their footage and add any special effects desired. Parental and community involvement was a key element of this project in terms of arranging interviews, obtaining advertisers, and conducting reporting/filming.

The Orange County Schools in Orlando, Florida offer a year-long television production class open to any interested high school student. Each class produces nine news show segments and a drunk driving commercial. Students also produce a nutrition music video, enter county media contests, and create a video "yearbook" of school activities.

Computers are used in all aspects of the writing and production process. The class emphasizes hands-on activities and involves very little lecture. Self- and peer-evaluation is used to judge the quality of work. Each news show is evaluated by all students involved in the production and a master list of all suggestions and critiques is posted for students to read and add their own comments. The journalism, yearbook, and newspaper classes write critiques for the television class to review. In addition, students can measure their success by entering their work in the county media contest—a "real world" evaluation.

Summary

Computers can support the teaching of the creative arts in a variety of ways. Many art and music teachers have discovered that computers allow creative students to accomplish a lot more than with traditional methods. Furthermore, the computer makes artistic pursuits accessible to students who would not otherwise try. For example, physically handicapped students can play musical instruments or draw using a computer through the use of an adaptive interface (see Chapter 12). It seems ironic that a tool originally developed as a supercalculator could ultimately make artists out of everyone!

Multimedia materials in the form of videodisc and CD-ROM are becoming increasingly common. Although they can be used across the curriculum, they have special relevance to the arts as a medium that can convey visual images, motion, and sound simultaneously. Art and music teachers are discovering that multimedia can get students excited about subjects that were previously perceived as deadly dull.

Finally, allowing students to make video productions links school with the television world and allows students to explore new kinds of creative skills, such as computer animation, script writing, and film editing.

Further Information

To learn more on computer graphics and animation, see Hill (1990), Foley et al. (1990), Newman & Sproull (1985), or Weinstock (1986). There are many books that provide guidance for doing art on specific computers, such as Gosney & Dayton (1989) or McClelland (1989). *Verbum* is a quarterly magazine that examines the use of computers as an artistic medium.

For more background about electronic music, see Boom (1987), Moore (1990), Roads (1987), or Yelton (1989). A number of magazines such as *Music Technology* and *Electronic Musician* publish the latest information about this field. The *Computer Musicians Source Book* includes a continually updated product directory and reprints of articles about electronic music.

Information about the companies that distribute videodiscs and CD-ROMs is provided at the end of Chapter 9.

References

Boom, M. (1987). *Music Through MIDI.* Redmond, CA: Microsoft Press.

Computer Musicians Source Book. Computer Musicians Cooperative, 30101 N. Sterling Ave., Peoria, IL 61604. (309) 685-4843.

Electronic Musician Magazine. 2608 Ninth St., Berkeley, CA 94760.

Foley, J., Van Dam, A., Feiner, S., & Hughes, J. (1990). *Computer Graphics: Principles and Practice (2nd edition).* Reading, MA: Addison-Wesley.

Gosney, M., & Dayton, L. (1989). *Making Art on the Macintosh.* Glenview, IL: Scott, Foresman & Co.

Hill, F. S. (1990). *Computer Graphics.* New York: Macmillan.

McClelland, D. (1989). *Painting on the PC.* Homewood, IL: Dow Jones Irwin.

Moore, F.R. (1990). *Elements of Computer Music.* Englewood Cliffs, NJ: Prentice-Hall.

Music Technology. Music Maker Publications, 22024 Lassen St., St 118, Chatsworth, CA 91311. (818) 407-0744.

Newman, W. M. & Sproull, R. F. (1985). *Principles of Interactive Computer Graphics (2nd edition).* New York: McGraw-Hill.

Park, C. (1985). *Interactive Microcomputer Graphics.* Reading, MA: Addison-Wesley,

Roads, C. (1987). *A History of Computer Music.* Los Altos, CA: William Kaufman.

Verbum (Journal of Personal Computer Aesthetics). P.O. Box 15439, San Diego, CA 92115-9868. (619) 233-9977.

Weinstock, N. (1986). *Computer Animation.* Reading, MA: Addison-Wesley.

Yelton, G. (1989). *Music and the Macintosh.* Atlanta, GA: MIDI America.

Activities

• If you are an art teacher, find different types of graphics programs and have your students experiment with them in the context of a specific assignment or project. Have them compare the relative merits of the different programs.

• If you are a music teacher, invite local musicians who use electronic instruments to come to class and demonstrate how they play. Take a field trip to a modern recording studio to examine how electronic technology and computers are used.

• For any teacher: Have your students make their own documentary as a class project. Break the project into parts so that everyone in the class has a role. (Borrow a camcorder from a friend if your school doesn't own one.)

Chapter 12
Special Needs

One of the most demanding kinds of teaching involves students with special needs—handicapped, disadvantaged, or gifted. Such students require additional attention and effort in terms of teaching methods and strategies. This is a domain in which technology can be of great value to teachers and students. It can provide instructional materials appropriate to students' specific needs. Specialized hardware and software can compensate for disabilities and allow students to learn as they wish.

Indeed, one of the major benefits of technology for the handicapped is to provide access to learning and education that previously was unavailable. Telecommunications networks provide the clearest example. Many students with physical, visual, or hearing disabilities are now able to participate fully in classes via electronic networks. In addition, special input/output devices and software allow handicapped individuals to use computers and the instructional or application programs discussed in this book.

Likewise, teachers with handicaps are able to overcome limitations that previously prevented them from achieving their full potential. Listen to what Professor Norman Coombs has to say about this:

Computer technology has drastically transformed my professional life both as a scholar and teacher. I am a blind professor of history at the Rochester Institute of Technology, and in recent years I have come to rely on a PC with speech synthesizer to assist me. Besides using word processing for writing handouts, memos, and professional articles, I connect with the university's main computer system using a modem and phone line. I found electronic mail could be used to have students send papers to me via the computer and have my speech synthesizer read them to me. One of the first to send me material through electronic mail was a hearing-impaired woman. After receiving her grade by return e-mail, she wrote back excitedly saying that this was the first time she had ever "talked" with a professor without needing an interpreter.

Source: From N. Coombs, "Computing and Telecommunications in Higher Education: A Personal View." *Educational Technology* (February 1990), p. 46.

Have Computer, Will Travel

Linda Copper is a full-time teacher for the Baltimore County Public Schools. She and her Apple IIc visit students who are confined at home or in hospital with broken legs, leukemia, brain tumors, head trauma, and a host of other disabilities that prevent them from attending a regular school-based program. She describes the results of her efforts:

The computer is used for a variety of purposes according to the subject, grade level, ability, and previous computer experience of each pupil. Younger children are introduced to the hardware and keyboarding, often for the first time. Software may be used to initiate a unit or topic, to motivate the student to learn a skill, or to explain a concept, sequence, or rule.

There is evidence that using a computer with confined children has positive effects. One example was an eighth grade learning disabled student who was having a difficult time with math. We used a software package on fractions and I would leave the computer in his home over the weekend for additional time. His comment was, "At last I really understand fractions, and all I had to do was break my leg." Being a captive audience in a body cast, the student used the time and opportunity to focus on the skill and he was eventually successful.

Two years ago, I taught a student who had a bone marrow transplant due to leukemia. He also had extensive chemotherapy. This child showed marked improvement, especially after using the computer twice a week for several months. Currently, I am teaching him his third grade curriculum because of the need for a second bone marrow transplant. We have just been notified that he scored 150 on the Otis-Lennon test and is being considered for the gifted and talented program next year.

One group of students shows very noticeable changes in response to the computer. This is the emotionally handicapped group. Their anxiety level decreases as they take control of an impersonal machine that guides them step by step at their own pace. They develop much more confidence and time on task increases. They begin to complete assignments and are able to transfer their learning to paper and pencil tasks. It is a beautiful and rewarding experience to see such a transformation!

One emotionally disturbed girl had been expelled from a special school due to explosive outbursts and aggressive behavior. As you might expect, she had a short attention span, low self-esteem, and an extremely low frustration level. She seemed to turn around when I introduced her to word processing on the computer: "This is fun and easy. I'll have to show this to my grandmother. I'll bet I could learn this at the high school or community college and get a good job." Being relaxed and at ease, she saw practical implications and even set a tentative goal on the spot. Small and insignificant? I don't think so—for this girl, a new way of thinking and a new direction! And the computer seems to affect this population of homebound students much the same way, regardless of age.

Tools for Communication

When special education teachers discuss the unique problems and needs of their students, the capability to communicate usually comes at the top of the list. Regardless of whether the handicap is a physical disability or a mental disorder, the use of technology to help students communicate better is one of the things that interests almost all teachers. Improving handicapped students' ability to communicate brings benefits in all their school and life activities.

Barbara Smith is a special education teacher at Glenmoor Elementary school in California. She works with severely disabled students from six to ten years old. Here is how she sees the value of computers:

All of my students have difficulty expressing themselves adequately and understanding everyday conversation at their age level. Even though we work on language throughout the day, new methods must be implemented to help the children converse appropriately with their peers. My goal in teaching language is to involve each child totally through visual, auditory, and kinesthetic modalities.

In the area of communication with nonverbal children, I have used communication books, gestures, and sign language. Communication books are often frustrating for the students, gestures work satisfactorily when used, and sign language does not enable them to communicate with peers. Since the Apple IIgs has a speech capability, pictures can be taken directly from the communication books, placed on a Unicorn keyboard, and messages programmed into the computer for each picture. When the students want to communicate with others, they simply touch the appropriate picture and the computer becomes their voice.

I have implemented a Special Friends program at Glenmoor. At lunch, third graders come to my classroom and pick up their special friend for lunch. They eat together and then play either outside or in the classroom. This leisure time is the perfect opportunity for using the computer to communicate. Leisure pictures can be put on the Unicorn keyboard and the students choose the play activity by touching the desired picture. I have also implemented a peer tutoring program at Glenmoor. Sixth grade students work as peer tutors in various areas of the curriculum throughout the day. Eight periods are specifically designated for computer activities. The peer tutor checks the computer folder to find out which programs are appropriate for individual students and then works with the student on a particular skill.

Computer technology has opened new worlds for people with disabilities. With the availability of talking software, speech synthesizers, touch-sensitive screens, and switches, as well as software designed specifically for the disabled, these students will be given new technological learning opportunities. I believe that all children can learn and that we are still learning through technology how to teach the most disabled.

Muriel Segal is a computer resource specialist for the Erie County Health Care Center for Children in Buffalo, New York. She explains how technology is used at this school:

Approximately 33 percent of the school population is neither physically able to speak nor possesses sufficient fine motor skills to sign. Many of our students are limited to using picture boards or Blyss symbol boards to communicate. These are extremely time consuming to create and inflexible to use. If severely handicapped students have just one set of controlled, predictable muscles they can use a switch attached to a computer via an Adaptive firmware card or the Aid + Me interface card with appropriate software. They can use this one device with a scanning program and commercial programs—a word processor, an educational program—to communicate, especially when a speech synthesizer such as the Echo has been installed.

Students with special musculature but not enough fine motor skills to use a standard keyboard can access an expanded keyboard such as the Unicorn or Powerpad. These aids can be individually programmed to meet the unique needs of each student and academic area. Words, sentence fragments, and complete sentences can be stored on floppy disks or the hard drive and downloaded into memory as needed. Special layouts can be designed to accommodate different learning styles, access methods, and levels of ability.

Word processing must be the centerpiece for our students. Magic Slate 20/40 is especially useful for children who cannot focus well enough to see 80 columns on the monitor. The simple commands delivered via both large letters and pictures will also help younger children just beginning to read and write. AppleWorks, a more complex program for children in grades 4-9, will meet their more sophisticated needs. The Timeout additions to AppleWorks provide many useful tools such as a spelling checker and calculator. Students can then do their arithmetic at the computer even though they could not access an ordinary calculator.

Because of the lack of communication skills, many of our students are quite passive in their relationships with fellow students and teachers—responding when addressed but seldom initiating conversation. If students absorb the technology to the point where they consider it their "voice" then we should see an observable and measurable change in this behavior. Students will participate more actively in class and in social situations.

Clearly these teachers feel that computers are especially valuable when used to enhance the communication capabilities of handicapped learners.

Learning Phonics

Laurie Fias is head of the language training department at Forman School in Litchfield, Connecticut. She describes a typical session with a dyslexic student using a Macintosh to learn phonics:

As with any lesson, in a class where the computer is the learning tool, the teacher takes certain steps to prepare the materials for class. For phonic lessons, she puts onto the class disk a file containing the sound/symbol correspondences for the day. If the student has a visual perceptual problem, she can make the symbols large. The teacher can work with the student to determine which typeface is easiest for him to read; fancy typefaces are not easily read and, although appealing to the nondyslexic, are not very useful for the dyslexic. As the teacher prepares the lesson for the student, the benefits of using the computer as a writing tool, so essential to the student, are realized by the teacher as well; she can arrange, rearrange, correct mistakes, etc. easily and save files for modification and use with another student at a later time.

When class begins, the student comes in and opens the file on the class disk with the day's work (the teacher may make it clear which file is to be opened by labeling it with that day's date). On the first page of the file, the student sees a list in 24 point type: ph, tch, ck, th, au, and aw. He reads each pair of letters aloud, pointing to them with the cursor as he does so. Underneath the list of letters, the student sees the word list for the day that the teacher has prepared (also in 24 point type if necessary): thatch, author, thaw, Auckland, rickshaw, phosphorus, hypothetical. As he reads the words, he tracks his progress through them by moving the cursor over the word.

After his list of words, the student sees a list of numbers followed by blank spaces. The teacher dictates a word and the student then spells it orally. When he has spelled it correctly, he clicks next to the first number and types in the word, spelling each letter as he strikes it on the keyboard. When he has finished, he proofreads what he has written, tracking over the word with the cursor to help him pay attention to each letter in the word.

Having made all corrections and put the day's work in a standard font size, the student prints out a clean copy of his work, revised and corrected, without the marks of revision appearing in the form of smeared ink, crossouts, erasure holes, or the like.

The same kind of techniques, highlighting, use of the cursor to track, increasing font size, utilizing the advantages of keyboarding for spelling and proofing, etc., and many others can be applied to the presentation of whatever new phonics material the teacher feels the student needs.

Source: From *The Macintosh Lab Monitor* (March 1990).

Students at Risk

One diverse group of students that has received considerable attention in recent years are so-called "at risk" or "Chapter One" students. Many schools have found that technology can get such students interested in learning and produce results that would not have been possible otherwise. Here are some examples taken from *K-12 Success Stories Guide for the Macintosh,* published by Apple Computer:

• A project called "Beyond the Limits" at Lincoln Junior High School in Kenosha, Wisconsin, involves the use of word processing and graphics software with a "writing across the curriculum" strategy. Students are given the chance to express themselves in their poetry and writing. Clip art is used as a springboard for creative writing. The students also use a video camera and MacVision to digitize images of themselves to illustrate autobiographies. At the end of the year they take the printed copies of their stories and create a book to share with other students, teachers, and parents. "Parents are overwhelmed at what the students are producing," says José Martinez, principal of the school. "The kids show their parents how they type in stories and scan pictures. They are able to teach their parents something, which really improves their self-esteem," he adds.

• At the Mid-Peninsula High School in Palo Alto, California, the emphasis is on having at-risk students use computers in nontraditional ways to make learning more interesting to them. Sakina Bush, the Learning Center instructor, explains: "We might have a kid who hates to write and needs the practice, but loves computer games. So we'd write a contract in which he or she agrees to produce a written set of instructions for a game after playing it for a week." If teachers find that students' reading difficulty is caused by poor ability in eyetracking, Sakina might work some computer time into their Learning Center activities. "They might read for fifteen minutes, work on Typing Tutor for ten minutes to develop their left-to-right eye tracking, then have a discussion with me. We use a variety of ways to get at a problem."

• At the Whittier Center in San Diego, California, deaf and hearing impaired students use HyperCard to write HyperStories—stories that let the reader choose the next turn of events. Students compose stories on a wide variety of topics using predefined templates. They may work as a group with different students writing different parts of the story. Hearing-impaired students may be paired with hearing students. According to Mary Lange, the teacher who developed the HyperStories idea, the language skills of the students have improved tremendously and the program has helped to identify language deficiencies that otherwise might have been overlooked.

• The Garnet Adult Education Center in Kanawha County, West Virginia, houses the county's School-Age Expectant Mothers program. Students remain in this program until their baby is born. However, after the birth they often drop out of school because they cannot afford child care or because they lose interest. Computers at the center can play many roles: strengthening basic skills through the use of drills and tutorial software; providing computer literacy in applications such as word processing and desktop publishing that could be valuable in getting a job; and contributing to instruction in parenting and family skills. Even though these students are not able to participate in regular schooling activities, technology can create meaningful and effective learning experiences.

HOTS for At-Risk Students

The Higher Order Thinking Skills (HOTS) project began in 1983 as an effort to develop a better approach to meeting the needs of at-risk students. A great deal of attention was being focused on this group of students, particularly through the use of computers for drill and practice in basic skills. The underlying concern was that "Chapter One" students were not doing well with existing programs, yet they seemed to possess a high degree of intelligence. The goal of the project was to develop a new thinking skills approach that would tap these students' intellectual potential in ways that would not only increase their thinking ability but also simultaneously increase their self-confidence and basic skills scores.

The fundamental question was: Could replacing all the supplementary drill with thinking activities "turn on" students intellectually in ways that improve basic skills and content learning? The answer to this question is a definite yes. Today the HOTS approach has been widely adopted and evaluated. Results show that HOTS is very effective and in many cases superior to conventional approaches to developing basic skills. In addition, HOTS techniques are also effective with other groups of students such as the learning disabled and the gifted and talented.

The essence of the HOTS approach is to provide students with regular and sustained thinking exercises (at least thirty-five minutes per day for two years) that are separate from classroom content and take place in social situations that are motivating and entertaining to students. The use of computers is an integral part of the HOTS program. However, computers are used to create "learning dramas"—opportunities for conversation or problem-solving activities. Almost any type of program (including drill and practice) could be used in a HOTS lesson, provided that it provokes discussion among students and teacher.

For more information, see S. Pogrow (1990), *HOTS: Using Computers to Develop Thinking Skills in Students at Risk.* (New York: Scholastic).

Summary

Many special education teachers are very enthusiastic about the potential of technology to improve the learning opportunities for handicapped and disabled students. One of the most important contributions that computers can make is to help such students improve their communication ability. In the case of at-risk students, computers can provide the means to make learning more interesting and rewarding for students who often find traditional school activities boring and irrelevant.

Although special interfaces and software are often needed for handicapped students, many of the classroom applications involved, such as word processing or desktop publishing, are the same ones discussed in earlier chapters. Similarly, the teaching techniques that seem to work best with handicapped students, such as cross-curriculum, cooperative learning projects, are the same ones that have been described by other teachers in this book. Technology may genuinely "close the gap" for teachers and students of all abilities.

Further information

There are some textbooks on the subject of special education and computers, but the following organizations, newsletters, and directories provide the most up-to-date information:

Apple Computer, Office of Special Education Programs, 20525 Mariani Ave., MS 36M, Cupertino, CA 95014. (408) 973-2732.

Center for Higher Education and Adult Training for People with Handicaps (HEATH), 1 Dupont Circle NW, Washington, D.C. 20036. (800) 544-3284.

Closing the Gap Resource Directory. Closing the Gap, Inc. P.O. Box 68, Henderson, MN 56044. (612) 248-3294.

Computers & the GT Student. Creative Computer Enterprises, 3002 Roanoke Cir., Lafayette, IN 47905. (317) 477-7306.

EDUCOM. *Computers and Students with Disabilities: New Challenges for Higher Education*. EUIT Program, EDUCOM, 1112 16th St. NW, Washington, DC 20036. (202) 872-4200.

IBM Corp. National Support Center for Persons with Disabilities. P.O. Box 2150, Atlanta, GA 30055. (800) IBM-2133.

LINC Associates. (1985). *SpecialWare Directory: A Guide to Software Sources for Special Education*. Oryx Press, 2214 North Central, Suite 103, Phoenix, AZ 85004-1483. (602) 254-6156.

The Macintosh Lab Monitor. Richard Wanderman, P.O. Box 1386, Litchfield, CT 06759. (203) 567-4307.

TRACE Research and Development Center, S-151 Waisman Center, 1500 Highland Ave., Madison, WI 53705. (608) 262-6966.

Activities

• Try using some basic skills software (e.g., vocabulary or math drills) with a group of handicapped students. Can you adapt the software to suit their needs? What changes to the programs would be necessary for it to work well with this group of students?

• Obtain some of the resource directories listed above and develop a plan for a "special needs" lab equipped with whatever hardware and software you think would be helpful to the students you work with. Can you find a company or parents who might sponsor such a lab and provide the funds needed to make it happen?

• If your school does not already use computer networks, investigate the possibility of getting access to one (see Chapter 5). Think about activities (such as writing, desktop publishing, or data collection) that handicapped students could participate in via the network. Revise existing lesson plans or create new ones to include such activities.

• This chapter has presented many positive examples of how technology can "close the gap" for handicapped individuals. Can you think of any opposite cases, i.e., situations in which technology could be detrimental to handicapped students or teachers?

Shape the world in which you live by creating your vision of reality

Chapter 13
Making Your Vision Happen

The purpose of this chapter is to help you think through the steps to make your vision about technology and learning become a reality. Visions about learning—from Sesame Street to SeniorNet—are described. The steps to follow include: developing a work plan, building a team, planning for implementation, and evaluation. There is also a section of evangelizing your idea to others. Our hope is that this chapter will inspire teachers to think creatively about the teaching/learning process and to have some direction in how to make their dreams become realities.

Research indicates that we teach the way we were taught. In our teaching, we must model the skills, knowledge and attitudes appropriate to the Information Age. These skills are as follows: organizing and sharing information, analyzing relationships, testing hypotheses, and communicating results. Many of the teachers who were profiled in this book are incorporating these skills into their work.

What Can Vision Accomplish?

In 1984 the authors of this book were engaged in the process of thinking through a vision—to examine how computers and telecommunications could enhance the lives of older adults. The result of their creative thinking was SeniorNet, a community of computer-using older adults (age 55-95). Seven years later, there are dozens of sites across the United States where older adults can take computer classes in word processing, telecommunications, and electronic citizenship (i.e., using computers and networks to fully participate in society). There is an online network connects the sites and over 4,000 SeniorNet members. On the network, members share tips about using computers, debate world issues, and provide a social/emotional support system. Members tell us that SeniorNet is a "community of the mind."

In 1969, Joan Cooney and Lloyd Morrisett asked whether television could help to educate preschool children. They assembled a team of educators to develop a set of learning objectives, which evolved into plans for television shows and ultimately became the Children's Television Workshop (CTW). Their most famous program, "Sesame Street" has fundamentally changed the nature of preschool education and our views about educational television.

Robert Tinker is interested in using computers to help students experience science firsthand. Tinker and other members of the Technical Education Research Center (TERC) in Cambridge, Massachusetts pioneered the development of Microcomputer-Based Labs (MBLs) and also have been instrumental in creating telecommunications networks for science teachers and students to collaborate on science experiments (see discussion in chapter 6). Here is how Tinker sees the significance of this technology to education in an editorial in *Hands-On!*:

> *We are entering the information age and telecomputing—the use of electronic networks for computer-based communications and information retrieval—is a virtual necessity that should be freely available to all students and teachers.*

Electronic mail, bulletin boards and conferences, remote bibliographies, and scientific databases already form the backbone of the information revolution and no child can be truly educated without familiarity with and access to these resources.

Tom Snyder was a teacher who could see the potential of computers in the classroom but was not impressed by the way in which they were used in most classrooms. He developed a new teaching approach (called the One Computer in the Classroom model) and new software to support it. Eventually, he started his own software company (Tom Snyder Productions) to develop and market this type of software. Here is how that goal is stated in the preface to *Teaching in the One Computer Classroom* (Dockterman, 1989):

The people who make up TSP (Tom Snyder Productions) are drawn together by a common philosophy: a vision of dynamic, interactive classrooms where students and teachers engage in the informed exploration of knowledge and ideas ... The computer can reduce the administrative burden teachers face; it can spark and help manage incredible class discussions; it can take a group of students on a field trip to a faraway world without ever leaving the classroom; it can provide teachers with a more powerful "chalkboard" than they ever imagined; it can do this and much more.

Snyder's teaching model and software are now used extensively in schools around the world.

The point of these examples is that a vision about the potential use of technology in education can have a significant impact on the lives of many students, either in a single school or in schools around the world.

Getting Started Can Be Difficult

This story by Lissa Rotundo, a high school biology teacher in Baltimore, Maryland, illustrates that the road to computerdom can be a rocky one:

Although I mastered word processing about ten years ago, until this summer I never dared to use a computer beyond that basic application. I attribute my computerphobia largely to a course called "Computers in the Science Classroom" that I took five years ago. We teacher-participants were expected to become computer-confident and competent by attending a daylong class each week, having no opportunities to practice out of class. A parade of "experts" came through, demonstrating a new technique each week. After each week, I fell further and further behind. As one of my fellow teacher-participants remarked:

"For once, I know what it feels like to be the slowest kid in the class and have everything go right over my head." I ended the course feeling totally unprepared to use computers in my classroom.

Given this background, it is understandable that when I was approached to participate in the multimedia project this summer, I was less than enthusiastic. What a difference eight weeks can make! The small class size (only three of us) and therefore ready access to the trainer's assistance kept frustration levels to a minimum. After an initial few weeks ascending a steep learning curve, I happily spent the remaining weeks creating animations that I am confident will enhance my ability to teach, and my students' ability to learn, the complex concepts of modern biology. By creating exactly the sequences I need to illustrate a point and having them do on the computer screen exactly what I want them to do, I can in a very direct way demonstrate to students what is happening in a given situation.

I feel that I have experienced significant growth as a teacher this summer. Many teachers at this stage of their careers are simply putting in time, teaching the same things, in the same way, that they have been teaching for years. In my view, multimedia computing is a promising tool that will give students and teachers a refreshing new way to learn and teach.

Developing a Work Plan

The first concrete step in realizing your vision is to create a work plan. The components of a work plan include: reconceptualizing the curriculum; determining the goals and objectives and sequencing the activities; understanding the social and educational context; placing the technology in context; planning for staff development; implementation; and assessing what your students produce. For each of these areas, you need to write specific plans that will help to achieve each task. Many teachers fail by having the vision but not thinking through the steps needed to implement their ideas. These include very specific tasks such as determining the software needed for desktop publishing; finding volunteer resource people to help students work with online databases; or convincing the school principal of the need for a phone line, modem, and telecommunications software for the classroom. These tasks need to be determined, sequenced, and attached to a plan that accounts for both time and financial resources.

Building Your Team

A key part of making your vision happen is building a team of people who can assist you. People who serve on your team include champions in helpful places—this could include your school principal, district superintendent, or a representative from industries in your community. Another part of the team are the "worker bees"—the people who can really make your idea happen. Students in the same age group as your students or older students can be a great help. Another group necessary to make change happen are your "investors." These are individuals, businesses, or foundations who "buy into your dream" and are willing and able to invest financial or human resources in making your dream become a reality. For example, the Apple Community Affairs program has invested in many of the ideas of teachers profiled in this book. They have provided equipment support and seed funding. Once the teachers received the initial support, they were usually able to leverage it to get other support (i.e., "matching grants") from other businesses in their community.

Many of the teachers interviewed for this book describe another necessary part of the team—the personal support system. Kathleen Duplantier (see Chapter 8) tells how her husband helped her to set up her computer lab of Macintoshes and videotaped her students engaged in their projects. He even produced a videotape for her to use in telling people about her project. Husbands, wives, parents, other teachers, and friends play an important role in providing the ongoing encouragement and "third hand" often needed.

Implementation: It's Not Easy!

When teachers attempt to implement fundamental changes in education, they must also revise their deeply held, traditional beliefs about schooling. In this book we have mentioned many of the new philosophies that go hand in hand with technology such as cooperative learning, cross-curriculum projects, qualitative assessment, and the like. The change process is difficult, requiring ongoing support from colleagues and administrators at each phase.

Technical training is vital in the beginning. Later, teachers need more opportunities to examine and discuss their actions and underlying beliefs, and freedom to explore new approaches and curricula. For example, in the Apple Classrooms of Tomorrow (ACOT) Project teachers evolved through five stages of change: awareness, adoption, adaptation, appropriation, and invention. Each stage involved different beliefs about the role and significance of technology in the classroom.

In the implementation phase, the work is not glamorous. It involves keeping an eye on the end goal while spending most of the time on monitoring progress and making sure everything is working properly. High school science teacher Russ Doren talks about his vision and the work he does each day to achieve it.

About five years ago, a student approached me about starting a student Macintosh User's Club at CCHS. After going through all the necessary procedures for official sponsorship, our club was formed. Our club has been active through the years, with membership numbers rising and falling. We have about half a dozen very active members at this point who are working to increase our membership ranks and get more kids involved. A few weeks ago, the students decided to spend club funds on software, particularly games including SimCity and Shanghai. Last year, the students purchased and donated software to our school's library including several clip art packages, WriteNow, and SuperPaint. Students can check out this software and use it on our library's Macintosh computers. Our library now has a Mac SE hooked to an overhead projector, so the kids want to start having software demos at our meetings.

For three of the last four years, the Mac Club members have also sponsored a MacVision portrait booth at our school's annual Oktoberfest. Our booth has always been very popular—the CCHS students really enjoy having the computer portrait booth. In fact, our school's library personnel have used the idea to operate a computer portrait booth at our school's after-prom party in the spring.

About five years ago, our school district decided to convert our entire film library from 16mm films to videotapes. Literally thousands of films have been replaced. Unfortunately, our school had very few video recorders on which to show the new videotapes. New district equipment had not been written into the plan. In order to help our department successfully keep up with changes in video technology, I spearheaded efforts to purchase and install a set of 27" high-resolution color monitors in three of our classrooms.

After several years of hard work, the monitor installation was completed November, 1989. Our pilot video program has created a great deal of interest in and out of the school and seems to have snowballed into efforts by other science department members to have monitors installed in their rooms. In fact, I have conducted at least four after-school demonstrations of our equipment to other departments and to other high schools in our district! Not only has the equipment been used for videotapes, it has also been used for an interactive computer videodisc system and two videomicroscope setups I helped establish.

I am especially proud of the videodisc program I initiated last year. I received a $2,000 district grant for instituting an interactive videodisc system in our department. The grant was entitled "Interactive Videodisc Technology in the Science Classroom—Tomorrow's Classroom Today" and involved the purchase of a hard drive for our Macintosh computer, a Pioneer LDV-4200 videodisc *player, and a BioSci videodisc with HyperCard stackware. The BioSci videodisc contains over 5,000 color slides covering at least seventeen different areas of biological science and can be used all year. I have compiled a number of slide shows on animal taxonomy and run my slide shows on specific animal groups while lecturing on details of each group as the slides are shown. I have also had great success using the videodisc for a discussion of cell division through the use of the disc's short film sequence on mitosis. Using a graphic remote control on the Mac's screen, I run the film backward and forward and also use stop action in order for the students to understand the process of mitosis thoroughly.*

I feel that interactive videodisc technology is here to stay. In fact, our advanced placement biology classes also use the interactive setup. We have written two more laserdiscs and stackware into our new year's budget and an upgrade to the BioSci videodisc we own now. Our library has also put together an interactive video system and plans to check it out to other departments in the school.

As a follow-up to the demonstrations of our interactive videodisc system, I will be running a districtwide workshop on videodisc technology in December, 1990. As a supplement to this workshop, I also plan to demonstrate digital video on the Mac (MacVision) and digital sound on the Mac (MacRecorder). I love digital sound on the Mac and have become a collector of digitized Macintosh sounds.

A project I undertook two school years ago was acting as registration chairman of our 1988 State Science convention. I initiated the use of the Macintosh for registration of attendees and the printing of legible, large-type badges. The use of the Mac was a resounding success and was also used by other teachers to help coordinate registration at [the] 1990 science convention.

Another project I tackled was our department's Physical Science Laboratory Activity book. Members of our department had accumulated labs over the years and had compiled a lab book, but wanted the book to have a more professional touch. Using a Macintosh computer, MacWrite, and a laser printer, I typed the 175-page book myself. Our physical science program went on to win an NSTA national award for being one of the top physical science programs in the country.

Over the last two years, I have seen a great deal of enthusiasm for the Macintosh from my colleagues. I share a converted classroom with five other teachers where I spearheaded the establishment of two Macintosh workstations and have hooked both Macs via phonenet to our school's laser printers. I am known as the "Mac techie" in our department and spend time helping colleagues solve any Mac problems. Of the six people in our office, four now own Macintosh computers at home (including myself). After I taught colleagues how to use the Mac, most have become ardent enthusiasts.

I have seen major changes in technology over the last sixteen years of teaching at Cherry Creek High School. I firmly believe that teachers who embrace all kinds of new technology can become better, more rounded teachers. I find that teaching in the classroom is more fun now than ever before, and I hope that I can do my part to share my ideas and enthusiasm with lots of different teachers.

With the world changing as rapidly as it has in the last decade, I feel that teachers have a duty to embrace the new technology that comes along and pass it on to their students. We owe it to the students to better prepare them for the real world beyond high school. I readily and enthusiastically accept the challenge!

Evaluation

The next step in your work plan is evaluating the results. Evaluation is both formative and summative. Formative evaluation involves assessing your progress as you go along. In this phase, you change the direction of a project depending on the results you are seeing. In the summative phase, you collect pre- and postdata to determine the actual outcomes of your work. There are many helpful books on the topic of evaluation to assist you in determining appropriate methods and instruments to use in evaluating your work (see references at the end of this chapter).

When people think of evaluation, they tend to think of quantitative measurement and statistical tests. Although there is a role for this type of assessment in many projects, the most important type of evaluation for most projects (certainly in the formative stage) is qualitative or descriptive measurement. Asking people to describe their reactions or opinions to what you are doing either in writing or on camera usually produces valuable information. Collecting samples of work completed or problems encountered is also useful in analyzing and documenting the results of a project.

Many people are reluctant to have others review or evaluate their work because they fear criticism or rejection. Ironically, criticism is the very thing that makes a project stronger and ultimately leads to success. Having to analyze your work in terms of its shortcomings or weaknesses provides a basis for improvement and further development.

Evangelism

The last stage of achieving your vision is to become an evangelist for it. This means that you use a variety of means to get more people excited about your idea. You invite the press, local television, or radio, to do a story about your project. You take the press clipping, make copies of it, and send it to members of the school board, parents, and other potential investors. You develop a presentation about your vision and your project and talk about it at local or national teacher meetings, for example, at the National Education Computing Conference. You submit stories about your work to magazines such as *The Computing Teacher, Electronic Learning,* or a professional journal in your subject area. You talk to the local computer users' group to get them excited about your project and enlist their support and help.

The final aspect of evangelism is when you inspire others—your colleagues and students—to become evangelists. They share their excitement about the learning process and add their own ideas. In this way more people will try to adopt your vision. The ultimate goal, of course, is to help others shape their own visions. We can learn from the teachers in this book, understanding their visions, studying their work plans, and examining their evaluation results. In this way we can change the shape of education and prepare students for the Information Age.

Seeing the Payoffs

Cathie Marriott, library media specialist in a middle school in Orchard Park, New York, says, "With information doubling every four years, if you don't know how to get the answers you're sunk." Her vision of students able to access information and think about what they find has led her to her role as innovator in her school district and region. She received the NYSC&TE Outstanding Educational Technologist award and conducts inservice programs throughout the western New York region.

Ten years ago her principal asked her to take charge of an Apple II+ computer provided by the Chapter II program. Since then she has had to be resourceful to find ways to keep her library media center up to date. First she helped get a teacher center grant to develop teacher expertise in technology. Then she borrowed equipment from the local school library system to put in her library. The teachers and students were so enthusiastic that they collected $6,000 to buy equipment for the library. Now she has borrowed a Mac with CD-ROM player from the Erie-Catt teacher center. For Computer Learning Month she organized a pep rally. They had a marching band, kids wrote cheers for the cheerleaders, and synthesized music was used to introduce students to the magic of computer and the upcoming computers learning month events.

Cathie acts as a consultant to other teachers in the school, helping them develop project-oriented activities for the students to learn information-handling skills. She says, "To ensure the incorporation of appropriate technologies and information skills, cooperative planning with the subject area teacher is of the utmost importance. We discuss objectives and expectations, list skills, and indicate who is responsible for each. We discuss procedures and sequencing. This gives organization to the project as well as guidelines to the cooperating teacher."

Cathie is particularly excited about activities that involve students who do not perform well academically. For example, students research what a local business does and then make up their own questions to ask when they go to visit the businesses. She finds that these children are intimidated by books but not by computers. They use electronic sources such as Grolier's electronic encyclopedia, Microsoft bookshelf, CD Reader's Guide. She says: "Kids are more willing to keep looking because the technology makes information so accessible. Now they're even checking paper indexes. It's fun!"

Cathie describes the dramatic effects of her collaborative efforts from a library/media specialist's perspective:

- It is not unusual to find all of the 100 library chairs filled during most periods of the school day.
- In the past four years, book circulation has tripled.
- Software use has shifted from "edutainment" programs to utility programs. AppleWorks and Homeworker are the two most requested programs.
- Student enthusiasm has intensified.
- Computer equipment is constantly in use.
- Teacher participation has dramatically increased during the past four years.
- Interest in research and information accumulation has been overwhelming.
- Use of selected software across grade levels and disciplines has been maximized.
- Exposure to new technologies has influenced student decisions for technological purchases with student funds. The equipment for the circulation system and one of the CD-ROM drives were purchased with student funds.
- Best of all, students have realized that school can be exciting when you have the opportunity to use technology as a tool.

Summary

What is your role as a teacher in the Information Age? You are the one who creates a vision for the future. It is up to you to create models for teaching and learning that will help children to cope, adapt, or shape the reality in which they will live as adults. In the Information Age it is crucial that we as teachers shape our world by bringing our visions to reality. Such visions need to include projects about people, not technology. There needs to be a change in the educational paradigm—a shift from focusing on the subject matter to focusing on the learner and the society he or she is about to enter. The teachers profiled in this book have visions about that society. The skills and projects that their students are engaged in help to prepare them for the Information Age.

Further Information

To learn more about evaluation in the context of technology, see Bennett (1987) or Flagg (1990). For some classic visions of educational change, see Neill (1970), Leonard (1968), Rogers (1969), or Skinner (1968).

Bennett, R. (1987). *Planning and Evaluating Computer Education Programs.* Columbus, OH: Merrill Publishing Co.

Dockterman, D. (1989). *Teaching in the One Computer Classroom.* Cambridge, MA: Tom Snyder Productions. (617) 876-4433.

Flagg, B. (1990). *Formative Evaluation for Educational Technologies.* Hillsdale, NJ: Lawrence Erlbaum.

Furlong, M., & Kearsley, G. (1990). *Computers for Kids Over Sixty.* SeniorNet, 399 Arguello Blvd., San Francisco, CA 94118. (415) 750-5030.

Hands-On! Newsletter published by the Technical Education Research Centers. TERC, 1696 Masssachusetts Ave., Cambridge, MA 02138. (617) 547-0430.

Kawasaki, G. (1991). *Selling the Dream.* New York: HarperCollins.

Leonard, G. (1968). *Education and Ecstasy.* New York: Delacorte Press.

Lesser, G. (1978). *Children and Television: Lessons from Sesame Street.* New York: McGraw-Hill.

Neill, A. (1970). *Summerhill: For and Against.* New York: Hart Publishing Co.

Rogers, C. (1969). *Freedom to Learn: A View of What Education Could Become.* Columbus, OH: Merrill Publishing Co.

Skinner, B. (1968). *The Technology of Teaching.* New York: Appleton-Century-Crofts.

Snyder, T., & Palmer, J. (1986). *In Search of the Most Amazing Thing.* Reading, MA: Addison-Wesley.

Activities

- Interview one or more teachers who are technology leaders in their school system. What is their vision of the role of technology in education? How does it compare to the visions described in this book?

- This chapter outlines a number of steps involved in realizing a vision. Which one do you feel is the most critical? Which one(s) do you feel most or least capable of accomplishing?

- Review the visions articulated by well-known educational reformers such as those cited in the references. How do the teacher visions about technology discussed in this book compare to theirs?

- Articulate your own vision of how technology could make a difference in teaching and make it happen!

Chapter 14
Learning More

This chapter provides additional sources of information about technology and education. There are many excellent books on all aspects of the topic that you can read for background and ideas. But be warned; because technology changes so quickly, it is difficult to stay up to date! To get the latest information, we recommend attending conferences, reading magazines or journals, and participating in online networks devoted to educational computing. We also recommend writing or calling software publishers for their latest catalogs.

Books

Here is a selected list of books (in addition to those cited in previous chapters) that deal with different aspects of technology and education:

Ambron, S., & Hooper, K. (1990). *Learning with Interactive Multimedia.* Redmond, WA: Microsoft Press.

Barker, P. (1989). *Multimedia Computer Assisted Learning.* New York: Nichols Publishing Co.

Bork, A. (1987). *Learning with Personal Computers.* New York: Harper & Row.

Bowers, C. A. (1988). *The Cultural Dimensions of Educational Computing: Understanding the Non-neutrality of Technology.* New York: Teachers College Press.

Campbell, P., & Fien, G. (1986). *Young Children and Microcomputers.* Englewood Cliffs, NJ: Prentice-Hall.

Clements, D. (1985). *Computers in Early and Primary Education.* Englewood Cliffs, NJ: Prentice-Hall.

Gluck, M. (1990). *HyperCard, Hypertext, and Hypermedia for Libraries and Media Centers.* Englewood, CO: Libraries Unlimited.

Haynes, G. R. (1989). *Opening Minds: The Evolution of Videodiscs and Interactive Learning.* Dubuque, IA: Kendall/Hunt.

Hohmann, C. (1990). *Young Children and Computers.* Ypsilanti, MI: High/Scope.

Johnston, J. (1987). *Electronic Learning: From Audiotape to Videodisc.* Hillsdale, NJ: Erlbaum Assoc.

Jonassen, D. (1989). *Hypertext/Hypermedia.* Englewood Cliffs, NJ: Educational Technology Publications.

Kearsley, G. (1987). *Artificial Intelligence and Instruction.* Reading, MA: Addison-Wesley.

Langhorne, M. J., Donham, J. O., Gross, J. F., & Rehmke, D. (1989). *Teaching with Computers.* Phoenix, AZ: Orynx Press.

Lathrop, A., & Goodson, B. (1984). *Courseware in the Classroom.* Reading, MA: Addison-Wesley.

Lawler, R., & Yazdani, M. (1987). *Artificial Intelligence and Education.* Norwood, NJ: Ablex.

Lillie, D. L., Hannum, W. H. & Stuck, G. B. (1989). *Computers and Effective Instruction.* New York: Longman.

McFarland, D. & Parker, O. R. (1990). *Expert Systems in Education and Training.* Englewood Cliffs, NJ: Educational Technology Publications.

Nix, D., & Spiro, R. (1990). *Cognition, Education, and Multimedia.* Hillsdale, NJ: Erlbaum.

Pea, R., & Sheingold, K. (1987). *Mirrors of Mind: Patterns of Experience in Educational Computing.* Norwood, NJ: Ablex.

Polson, M.C., & Richardson, J. J. (1988). *Foundations of Intelligent Tutoring Systems.* Hillsdale, NJ: Erlbaum Associates.

Riedesel, C., & Clement, D. (1985). *Coping with Computers in Elementary and Middle School.* Englewood Cliffs, NJ: Prentice-Hall.

Roblyer, M. D, et al. (1988). *The Effectiveness of Computer Applications for Instruction: A Review and Synthesis of Recent Research Findings.* New York: Hawthorn.

Simonson, M., & Thompson, A. (1990). *Educational Computing Foundations.* Columbus, OH: Merrill Publishing Co.

Turner, S. & Land, M. (1988). *Tools for Schools: Applications Software for the Classroom.* Belmont, CA: Wadsworth.

Van Horn, R. (1990). *Advanced Technologies in Education.* Belmont, CA: Wadsworth.

Vockell, E., & Schwartz, E. (1988). *The Computer in the Classroom: Enhancing Academic Learning Time.* Santa Cruz, CA: Mitchell Publishing Co.

Wenger, E. (1986). *Artificial Intelligence and Tutoring Systems.* Los Altos, CA: Morgan Kaufmann.

Willis, J., Hovey, L. & Hovey, K. (1987). *Computer Simulations: A Sourcebook to Learning in an Electronic Environment.* New York: Garland Publishing Co.

Organizations

A number of national organizations are concerned exclusively with technology and education. They all hold annual conferences and have their own publications.

• Association for the Advancement of Computing in Education (AACE). P.O. Box 2966, Charlottesville, VA 22902. (804) 973-3987

Formed in 1989 to encourage scholarly inquiry related to computers and education. Publishes *Journal of Computing in Childhood Education*, *Journal of Computers in Mathematics and Science Teaching*, *Journal of Artificial Intelligence in Education*, and *Journal of Educational Multimedia and Hypermedia*.

• Association for the Development of Computer-based Instructional Systems (ADCIS) 229 Ramseyer Hall, 29 W. Woodruff Ave., Columbus, OH 43210. (614) 292-7900

The oldest organization devoted to the field of computer-based education and training. Has special interest groups on all aspects of CBI and holds an annual conference in November. Publishes *Journal of Computer-Based Instruction*.

• Association for Educational Communications & Technology (AECT) 1025 Vermont Ave. NW, Washington, D.C. 20005. (202) 347-7834

Dedicated to the application of educational technology to the learning/teaching process at all educational levels. Sponsors an annual conference. Publishes *Educational Technology Research & Development* and *Tech Trends*.

• International Society for Technology in Education (ISTE). University of Oregon, 1787 Agate St., Eugene, OR 97403. (503) 686-4414

Focused on the interests of K-12 teachers and technology. Represents Computer-Using Educator (CUE) groups around the world. Sponsors the annual National Educational Computing Conference (NECC) in June. Publishes *The Computing Teacher* and *Journal of Research on Computing in Education*.

• EDUCOM. 1112 16th St. NW, Washington, DC 20036.(202) 872-4200.

Supports the use of computers at the college and university level. Holds an annual conference in October. Publishes *EDUCOM Review*, a quarterly newsletter. Also coordinates BITNET, an international computer network.

Magazines

Here are some commercial magazines that focus on technology in education:

• *Educational Technology*. 720 Palisade Ave., Englewood Cliffs, NJ 07632. (201) 871-4007.

• *Electronic Learning.* 902 Sylvan Ave., Englewood Cliffs, NJ 07632. (212) 994-770.

• *Teaching and Computers.* Scholastic, Inc., 730 Broadway, New York, NY 10003. (212) 505-3000.

• *Technology & Learning.* Peter Li Inc., 19 Davis Dr., Belmont, CA 94002. (415) 592-7810.

• *T.H.E. Journal.* Information Synergy, Inc., 2626 S. Pullman, Santa Ana, CA 92705. (714) 261-0366.

Computer Networks

There are literally hundreds of computer networks and online services that are relevant to education. Here is a sampling of some national networks:

• America Online. Quantum Computer Services, 8619 Westwood Center Dr., Vienna, VA 22182. (800) 227-6364.

An online information utility that features e-mail, special interest groups, news, and technical support groups. Has special area for educators.

• AT&T Long Distance Learning Network, 295 North Maple Ave., Room 6234S3, Basking Ridge, NJ 07201. (800) 367-7225; (201) 221-8544.

An electronic mail system used to link schools in online learning circles.

• BreadNet. Bread Loaf School of English, Middlebury College, Middlebury, Vermont 05753. (802) 388-3711.

Supports teachers who have taken part in the summer writing programs run by the college

• CompuServe. 5000 Arlington Center Blvd, Columbus, OH 43220. (800) 848-8199; (614) 457-8600.

The largest commercial online network. Features a number of educational forums.

• DIALOG. Dialog Information Services, 3460 Hillview Ave., Palo Alto, CA 94304. (800) 334-2564; (415) 858-2700

The largest of the commercial online database vendors. Offer curriculum materials and software for introducing students to online databases.

• Dow Jones News/Retrieval Service. P.O. Box 300, Princeton, NJ 08543. (800) 552-3567; (609) 520-8349.

The largest commercial vendor of online news and financial databases. Offer special flat rates for schools and a curriculum guide.

• FrEdMail. FrEdMail Foundation, Box 243, Bonita, CA 92002-0243. Modem: (619) 475-4852.

A network of bulletin boards that allows schools across the country to exchange files.

• Kids Network. National Geographic Society, Educational Media, 17th and M Sts. NW, Washington, DC 20036. (800) 638-4077.

Curriculum materials for middle school that involve collaborative data collection via networks.

• Learning Link. LinkNet, 1400 E. Touhy Ave., Suite 260, Des Plaines, IL 60018. (708) 390-8700.

Provides information about educational television offerings, especially PBS programs.

• SpecialNet. GTE Education Services, 8505 Freeport Pkwy, Suite 600, Irving, TX 75063. (800) 634-5644.

Dedicated to the needs of special education teachers and administrators

---

Software Publishers/Distributors

Borland International, 1800 Green Hills Rd., Scotts Valley, CA 95066. (408) 438-5300.

Brøderbund Software, 17 Paul Dr., San Rafael, CA 94903. (800) 521-6263.

Brooks/Cole Publishing Co., 511 Forest Lodge Rd., Pacific Grove, CA 93950. (408) 373-0728.

EduCorp, 7434 Trade St., San Diego, CA 92121. (800) 843-9497.

Hiezer Software, 1941 Oak Park Blvd, Suite 30, P.O. Box 232019, Pleasant Hill, CA 94523. (415) 943-7667.

HyperGlot Software Co., 505 Forest Hills Blvd., Knoxville, TN 37919. (615) 558-8270.

IBM Corp., PC Software Sales, 1 Culver Rd., Dayton, NJ 08810. (800) IBM-2468.

Intellimation, P.O. Box 1922, Santa Barbara, CA 93116-1922. (800) 346-8355.

K-12 MicroMedia Publishing, 6 Arrow Rd., Ramsey, NJ 07446. (201) 825-8888.

Key Curriculum Press, P.O. Box 2304, Berkeley, CA 94702. (800) 338-7638

The Learning Company, 6493 Kaiser Dr., Freemont, CA 94555. (800) 852-2255.

MacroMind, 410 Townsend St., Suite 408, San Francisco, CA 94107. (415) 442-0200.

Microsoft Corp., One Microsoft Way, Redmond, WA 98052-6399. (800) 426-9400.

Minnesota Educational Computing Corp. (MECC), 3490 Lexington Ave. N., St Paul, MN 55126. (800) 228-3504.

Prescience Corp., 939 Howard St., Suite 100, San Francisco, CA 94103. (415) 543-2252.

Scholastic, 2931 E. McCarty St. Jefferson City, MO 65102. (800) 541-5513.

Sunburst Communications, 101 Castleton St., Pleasantville, NY 10570. (800) 628-8897.

Teacher Support Software, 1035 N.W. 57th St., Gainsville, FL. 32605 (904) 332-6404.

Tom Snyder Productions, 90 Sherman St., Cambridge, MA 02140. (800) 342-0236.

TrueBASIC, 12 Commerce Ave., West Lebanon, NH 03784. (800) 872-2742.

Vernier Software, 2920 S.W. 89th St., Portland, OR. 97225. (503) 297-5317.

William K. Bradford Publishing Co., 310 School St., Acton, MA 01720. (800) 421-2009.

Wings for Learning, 1600 Green Hills Rd., Scotts Valley, CA 95067. (800) 321-7511.

Wolfram Research, P.O. Box 6059, Champaign, IL 61821. (217) 398-0700.

Glossary

Animation: Use of computer graphics to create motion sequences on the computer or videotape. (Chapter 6, 7, 11)

Adaptive interface/firmware: Input or output device (such as a special keyboard, toggle switch, text-to-speech synthesizer) that allows a handicapped person to use a computer. Often involves both hardware and software. (Chapter 12)

Apple Computers of Tomorrow (ACOT): Project initiated by Apple Computer in 1987 that involved providing all teachers and students at participating sites with a computer at school and home. (Chapter 13)

Bulletin Board System (BBS): A telecommunications program that allows many people to sign on to the same computer and post or exchange messages. Also called a remote bulletin board system (RBBS). (Chapter 5)

Clip art: Electronic images (drawings, illustrations, decoration) that can be copied from a disk and used in documents. A graphics program is usually needed to load and work with clip art. (Chapters 4, 11)

Compact Disk-Read-Only Memory (CD-ROM): The use of compact disks to store information in digital form so it can be accessed by computers.

Cut and paste: The capability to copy electronic information (text, graphics, sound) from one part of a computer file to another. (Chapter 3)

Dots per inch (dpi): A unit of measurement commonly used to describe the quality of printed output (especially from a laser printer). (Chapter 4)

Database: Information stored in computer files, divided into sets of records with specified fields. Online databases are files that are accessible by telecommunications and networks. (Chapter 5)

Digitizing: Converting a graphic or sound sequence into electronic form. (Chapters 4, 9)

HyperCard: A hypermedia authoring tool marketed by Apple Computer for the Macintosh computer. (Chapter 10)

Hypertext/Hypermedia: Databases in which the information is organized and accessed via links among elements. In hypertext, the information is text only; in hypermedia it can be graphics, video, or sound. (Chapters 10, 11)

Liquid Crystal Display (LCD) panel: A device used in conjunction with an overhead projector that can project a computer screen on a wall for group viewing. (Chapter 2)

Local Area Network (LAN): A group of computers that are connected together directly by cables and without the use of telecommunications.

LOGO: A programming language for children originally developed at MIT. (Chapter 10)

Microcomputer-Based Laboratory (MBL): Use of a personal computer to collect and analyze data from field observation or experiments. (Chapter 6)

MIDI: A computer programming language for music. (Chapter 11)

Multimedia: Using computers to store and present text, graphic, photographic, video, and sound information. Videodisc or CD-ROM is typically used as the storage medium. See also Hypertext/Hypermedia. (Chapter 10, 11)

Operating system: The software that manages all input/output and file operations for a computer (e.g., MS-DOS, Unix). (Chapter 2)

Public domain software: Programs that are made available at no charge and distributed by computer user groups or on bulletin board systems. (Chapter 5)

Scanners: Devices that allow printed text and graphics to be converted to electronic form (digitized). (Chapter 4)

Stacks: HyperCard files or programs. (Chapter 10)

Supercomputer: A large high-performance computer usually shared by many users at or across institutions. (Chapter 6)

Telecomputing: Use of telecommunications networks to access computers and online databases. (Chapter 5)

Templates: Pre-formulated worksheets for specific tasks that can be loaded into integrated programs such as AppleWorks or Microsoft Works. (Chapter 2)

User Interface: The control functions that determine how you interact with a particular program. (Chapter 10)

Videodisc: An optical storage medium that allows multimedia information to be accessed by computers. (Chapters 6, 9, 11)

Index